MW01035964

# Praise for *A Canine Exposé*

*(Unbiased, random, unsolicited comments from readers)*

---

"Excellent book. The way Behnken captures dogs' traits is genius. Hansen's illustrations are spot on. A must read for all."

***I. Fisch, Renner, SD (Barry's brother-in-law)***

"Loved it, loved it, loved it! Buy it. Read it."

***C. Sekshun, Prairie du Sac, WI (Barry's sister)***

"Hansen's illustrations are addictive, realistic, clever and fun. Behnken's commentary is irresistible."

***J. Byrd, Mauston, WI***
***(Barry's summer camp swimming class 'buddy')***

"The wit is obvious and habit forming, can't wait for their next book."

***W. Pleasure, Clearwater, FL (Barry's college roommate)***

"Of all the books I have read, this one's clearly the better. I know you'll like it too."

***Y. Knott, Sister Bay, WI (Barry's good friend)***

"Absolutely brilliant work; entertaining, hilarious, educational, touching."

***J. Walker, San Diego, CA (Barry's college classmate)***

"Fantastic book. For the love of God, get it and read it!"

***Rev. B. Goode, Fox Point, WI (Barry's pastor)***

"I read it three times. It's that good. Still giggling."

***Q. Peedahl, Grafton, WI (Barry's granddaughter)***

"It's a real page turner, couldn't stop reading…or laughing."

***G. Perscreepers, Scottsdale, AZ (Barry's high school classmate)***

"Mmm, Mmm good, that's what this fun book is, Mmm, Mmm good."

***B. Haive, Westlake, OH (Barry's good friend)***

# A Canine Exposé

*A Guide to Different Breeds*

*with Commentary on*

*Why You Should Never Own One*

**By Barry Behnken**
**Illustrations by Emily Hansen**

# A Canine Exposé

*A Guide to Different Breeds with Commentary on Why You Should Never Own One*



First Edition


**Disclaimer**
In the event you use any of the information in this book for yourself, which is your constitutional right, the author and the publisher assume no responsibility for your actions.

Cover illustrations by Emily Hansen

ISBN: 979-8-9888400-0-8

Arthur Mae Publishing
Mequon, Wisconsin (USA)

# Dedication

*To Bonnie, Brian, Emily, Laura, Tor, Rachel, Benjamin, Hannah, Sofia, Kyra and Evan.*

*(Yup, you guessed it, that's our family. All their names are in the book. Can you spot them?)*

*Also, Susan, Jim and Donna.*

*(Yup, they're in here too.)*

---

## Dogs in our family

Yes, some of our family members have dogs. How else would I know so much about not caring for dogs?

Here's a small 'Shout Out' to these rescue dogs in our family.
Let's hear it for:

Blu
Cooper
Daisy
Hunter
Joy
Lucy

(And, yup, they are in here, too.)

# Contents

# Introduction

My daughter Emily and I share a great love of humor. When together, we usually try to make each other laugh. This can become a competition at times, each trying to 'out funny' the other. Emily (who *is* a dog lover) is also a very good artist and has created many paintings/drawings using various media. We have several of her pieces displayed in our home.

She is especially good at drawing dogs and birds. One day we had the idea to write and illustrate a parody book. We chose dogs and a guide to different breeds. (FYI, Emily used colored pencils for these illustrations.)

Watch out for what you try, sometimes it can lead to a lot of work, research, consultation, camaraderie, and pure fun.

I know there are many books 'out there' and our book will likely get lost in the morass of paperbacks and hardcovers. The new books are becoming very specific as the 'general' subjects have already been written about ad nauseam.

I have seen new very specific books in the **FOOD** category…for example:
*"Savory poppy seed recipes for Thursday dinners."*
*"Vegan sides for your filet mignon entree."*

In the **HEALTH** category:
*"Finger pushups to strengthen palm muscles."*
*"30 days to lower blood pressure using Adriatic sea salt."*

In the **WELLNESS** category:
*"The Uff Da meditation for Norwegian librarians."*
*"Violet-colored lavender candles for calming a February 29 fear."*

In the **SPORTS** category:
*"Picking up the 8-10 split."*
*"Backyard bocce with only 7 large balls."*

Do you see what I mean? There are books of all kinds, but would you buy them and read them? We thought long and hard about attempting this as we wanted our book to be clever, funny, educational, heartwarming and a page turner. After much consideration we concluded, "What the hell, let's give it a shot."

While compiling this book, I was often asked "What kind of book is it?" I would always reply: "It's in the humor category. A parody which reads like a stream of consciousness, stand-up comedy routine, by a non-dog loving curmudgeon, with tongue in cheek and clever illustrations."

We had three objectives in writing *A Canine Exposé*:

1. To make people laugh and enjoy this parody which uses our quirky sense of humor.
2. To enlighten readers with some fun dog facts.
3. To challenge readers to use their brains. Use it or lose it is a real thing for brain health. Neuroplasticity is the ability of the brain to change through use. Use yours! Curiosity is a mainstay of brain exercise. We offer opportunities to be curious. Think about, wonder about and research different subjects included herein.

As an example, what is an 'Elizabethan Collar?' What is it used for?
Or, what is Occam's Razor? What does it mean? Who was Occam?
Or, what does *de rigueur* mean? Where did the phrase come from?
Or, is merle really a color? Or fawn or brindle, for that matter.
Don't just read the book. Wonder and learn about anything that piques your interest. You'll be happy as dog with two tails if you do.

(**Author's Note:** This book is intended to be a funny and enjoyable parody about dogs and dog owners. If you are offended by it, please stop reading and move on with your life.)

(**Another Author's Note:** The final editing of this book yielded one misspelling. We left it in. Can you fnid it?)

# Acknowledgements

I have the absolute greatest wife on the planet. (I've been in love with her since kindergarten.) Being an elementary school teacher in her early life, Bonnie has dogged me to be better at grammar. I guess I never knew what an adverb was until I met her. Much to my delight, she continues to hound me about my occasional grammatical missteps. Who better to be a proofreading editor? And I thank her for it and her support as we cranked through this absolutely fun process.

Emily provided fantastic drawings and also used her proof-reading expertise along the way. (She is a dog lover. For proof, read her *Ode to Blu* at the end of this book.)

Our son Brian offered insights on early drafts and we're grateful for his patience tolerating our many discussions. (Plus, he has three grand dogs.)

Mike Dauplaise and Bonnie Groessl of M&B Global Solutions acted as advisors, designers and contributed greatly towards the publishing of this book. Their expertise in all things technical and digital is appreciated.

Thanks to all the friends that reacted positively when I told them about this book. They helped motivate me to proceed.

# Pets in General

You may have figured out that I am not a dog person. It will become quite obvious as you read on.

We had a dog once for over two years. He was a yellow Labrador Retriever named Leo. Before we got him, he had been trained to bird hunt, but we were not hunters, we were more like gatherers, or shoppers. Two working adults and two school age kids meant Leo stayed home alone all day. Due to separation anxiety, he started licking his front paws raw. To prevent this, our veterinarian recommended we place a plastic utility bucket (with a hole in the bottom) on his head while he stayed alone all day, à la the Elizabethan Collar or 'Cone of Shame.'

When one of us came home, he was so excited that he ran and jumped around in joy as he flung droplets of urine about with reckless abandon. We let him out to do his business all winter in Wisconsin. When spring came, and the snow melted, our yard looked like there had been an explosion in a Lincoln Logs® factory out there. Bonnie and I couldn't do this with or to him any longer, so she drove him back to the farm of his breeder. She graciously accepted him back for a much better life. When we told the kids that Bonnie had taken Leo to 'The Farm,' they mistakenly thought we had him 'put down.' To this day, in our family, taking or sending something 'To the Farm' means it has been put out of its misery.

Pets are either expensive ($$) OR very expensive ($$$$) and they are very messy (***)

***Note:*** *As a convention for this book, when discussing an issue regarding dogs, anything that will cost the owner money will be indicated ($$$), and anything that describes a messy issue will be indicated (***).*

This book only discusses dogs. Don't get me started on other animals that people keep as pets:

- Cats, Meh, (that's meh not mew.)
- Rodents (ever heard of the bubonic plague?)
- Fish (clean the filter, scoop out the dead ones, scrape the algae.) ($$$) and (***)
- Rabbits (try to keep the number down, if you can.)
- Birds (feathers everywhere, incessant chirping.) ($$$) (***)
- Reptiles (are you kidding me?) Never could understand snakes. I hate snakes.

St. Patrick was OK by me.

# Doggie Discharge (***)

Dogs emit, shed or spew many substances, each more disagreeable than the other. Here are a few to be aware of. (Doggonit, I ended that sentence with a preposition.) I'll change it for you, if that would be OK? (Oh no, now I ended it with a proposition.)

**Hair (***)**

Most dogs shed (***) and those that don't, need to have haircuts ($$$). Shedding dogs can leave hair everywhere. Oh, our neighbor Hannah brought us a nice pasta casserole. Dollars to donuts her Border Collie was in the kitchen when she made it. We can tell by the black connecting strands between several pieces of the penne.

Or "Those are nice slacks Rachel; you must have an Irish Setter."
Think 'Lint Rollers' in every room and the car. To find a nice collection of dog hair, check the dryer screen, there should be about a bale in there.

**Saliva (***)**

Can we talk about dog saliva? (***) My least favorite liquid of all time. A semi-translucent, somewhat viscous, nearly colorless liquid which can be found on dogs' tongues, mouths and noses. You can tell exactly where your nephew's Lab sniffed your crotch by the gooey nose print on the front of your khakis.

It also can be seen hanging from the corners of a dog's mouth in various lengths which can whip around and catch on items as the dog turns or shakes his head. "Hey Milo, over here!" and with a whip of his head the slobber has hooked onto Grandma Susan's favorite Christmas ornament and snatched it right off the tree. Try getting that off a vintage, flocked, fragile, hollow glass ball with an image of Jesus on it. Oy Vey!

What an interesting substance, it seems to cling together and to other objects like it has a magnetism or something. It does not evaporate, nor can it be removed from objects using everyday cleaning procedures. Too bad 3M® didn't invent it and convert it into a useful commercial product. If you don't have a dog, you won't have this issue, except, of course, with other people's dogs.

**Breath (***)**

Yes, dogs can have bad breath too, and most do. Try not to get too close to them if you have a queasy stomach. It's another reason not to kiss a dog. For humans, we can re-brush our teeth, use mouthwash or breath fresheners. Bart the Golden, however, just exhales and doesn't care where it goes. If indoors, you're screwed, when outdoors, stay upwind.

**Urine (***)**

Oh, urine, a necessary but nasty liquid. It stains carpet, kills grass and reeks. If you don't think dog urine is a problem, consider this; a Google search for "How to get dog pee, smell and stains out of carpet" yielded 87,500,000 results (in 0.55 seconds). And that's just carpet! To say nothing of sofas, wallpaper, pillowcases, wedding dresses, onesies or blue suede shoes.

Male dogs don't seem to care as they prance around flinging droplets of pee willy-nilly, on the wall, on the shower curtain, on Grandma Laura's walker.  Even more so when they're excited.

When outdoors, dogs pee on almost everything. Aside: (sotto voce) I sometimes find myself hoping 'some' people I don't care for, will be reincarnated as a fire hydrant or mailbox post.

**Dog Doo (***)**

What to call it? This is a dilemma. It can be called doo, crap, poop, turds, No.2, waste and so on. (I tried not to use the S word in this book, but I did once. Can you find it?)

What more to say about it. Everyone has experience with it. As kids we ran barefoot and had it squish up between our toes. Later in life, it filled in the gaps on the bottom of our 'waffle stompers' and we tried, unsuccessfully, to dig it out with a small twig.

Everyone knows this scenario. Several people are walking along outside, when suddenly all smell that unmistakable odor and immediately everyone is checking the bottom of his shoes. You know the drill. And voila, Brian has the nasty on the bottom of his Allen Edmonds®.

It is a most controversial subject between dog people and non-dog people. "Don't let your dog crap in my yard," etc. Have you seen the little yard signs showing a squatting dog with a large red X or one of those 'Cancel' symbols on it? That's tacit dog doo warfare.

Also remember, your crapping canine needs to be 'walked' a couple of times daily. 'Walking' is a euphemism for letting it find a place to take a pee and a dump. This activity is OK for the owner on nice sunny days, but the weather doesn't always cooperate. You must also 'walk' it at 100 degrees F with 95% humidity or at 10 degrees below zero with a 20-mph wind or my biggest chuckle—during a sleet/snow storm with 3 inches of slush on the ground.

This must be Mother Nature's way of concurring that dogs are too much trouble.

**Puke (***)**

Yes, dogs can have sensitive upper GI systems too. Have you ever seen one yacking to get something out of its gullet? Maybe a partially rotted pigeon, or some dead animal entrails. Aren't they offal?

I heard of a dog who had so many vomiting episodes the owner trained it to jump into the bathtub to puke. That made cleaning it up a little easier, but it didn't work out so well for Aunt Sofie when she was taking her afternoon bubble-bath.

**Flatulence (***)**

Dogs fart just like people. Although some people claim they don't. I've seen research that says people fart an average of 14 times a day. (Who did this research, anyway? If it was done via self-reporting, you can bet the number should have been inflated.) Dogs can clear a room with a silent, but deadly, emanation. I suppose the only good thing about a farting dog is that your Uncle Jimmy can blame the dog, if anyone believes him.

# Paraphernalia Required For Dog Ownership ($$$$)

Have you been in a pet supply store? My God, there are millions of products for dogs, all of which you should own ($$$) if you want to be considered a 'good and proper' dog owner.

I get that you should have a collar, a leash and probably some food but, geeez...Here's an example of how crazy we have gotten. One pet supply company advertises products in these categories for dog clothing! CLOTHING!

- Dog Boots, Shoes & Socks (52 items)
- Dog Dresses (22)
- Dog Onesies & Dog Pajamas (41)
- Dog Shirts & Tank Tops (151)
- Dog Sweaters & Hoodies (195)
- Dog Life Jackets & Swimsuits (SWIMSUITS?) (12)
- Dog Coats & Jackets (293)
- Dog Costumes (19)
- Dog Jerseys & Team Apparel (302)

An internet search for supplies needed for a new dog only yields the following:

- Dog food
- Food and water bowls
- Leash
- Collar I.D. Tag
- Shampoo
- There is no mention of clothing!

*(**Author's Note:** The only 'clothing' for dogs that makes sense to me is the booties that the Iditarod mushers put on the dogs to prevent foot damage from the icy surface they run on for many days.)*

# Dog People vs Non-Dog People

By now you believe I am not a dog person. Besides the cost ($$$) and mess (***), dogs are a 24/7/365 nuisance, and no, you don't get February 29 off.

I do like certain other people's dogs at their house. I've been known to pet a dog or scratch it behind the ears, if a source of soap and hot water are nearby and if they haven't been trying to hump my leg. I don't want the cost, hassle or mess associated with a dog. It's as simple as that.

Dog People, on the other hand, drive with dogs in their lap, pull them in carts behind their bikes, kiss their dogs (apparently unaware of cystic echinococcosis or hydatid cysts), carry them on stairways, and trip unsuspecting shoppers at crowded farmers' markets with a network of leashes. Now I know why the Baha Men wondered "Who Let the Dogs Out?"

Some people actually resemble their dogs. Just wondering...does the person buy a dog that looks like her or does she change herself to look like the dog? I'll go with Occam's Razor on that question. You know, the simplest explanation—some dog people are nuts.

Many dog people bring their dogs to a hotel...and the hotel *allows* them stay! Apparently, the hotel management assumes I'm going to be OK occupying a room that previously housed a dog. I've seen the perfunctory effort that housekeeping staffs exert when cleaning rooms. I'm not sitting on that couch where Buffy was scooting last night. Or using *that* pillow!

Yet another example of dog people. I go for a walk quite often. When out on streets or sidewalks, I occasionally get challenged by someone's dog, a situation I don't appreciate. If the owner isn't around, this can be quite unnerving and I'm looking for some type of defensive weapon. Stick? Rock? If the owner is nearby, she may notice the snarling behemoth slowly approaching me with teeth bared, ears pinned back against the head, and tail high and arched over the back. Me? I'm about to soil myself, but she attempts to allay my obvious fear with the following: "Oh, don't worry, he's friendly, he doesn't bite."

Friendly? Doesn't bite? I can see his teeth. Does he gum his food? How does he consume his food, just swallow it whole?

I looked up the definition of 'Tooth.' Kind of hard to conclude he doesn't bite when teeth are defined as hard structures on the jaw and in the mouth used for catching and masticating food and as weapons of offense and defense. Another definition includes something that injures, tortures, devours or destroys. Doesn't bite? Having teeth includes being a *de facto* biter. But I'd better stop the biting commentary. I'll just let the reader chew on this a bit.

Here's another difference between dog people and non-dog people. As a non-dog person out for a walk, I meet my neighbor Evan and his dog, Daisy. He's swinging a small colored bag of dog doo in one hand. He can stand and talk to me for a long time, holding a bag of dog crap. Later, I don't remember any of the conversation with him because all I could think is, "HE'S HOLDING A BAG OF DOG CRAP!" (***)

I get a kick out of watching dog owners do the dog doo pick up with the bag. Hand inside the bag, grab the steaming pile, invert the bag while removing from the hand, being careful not to contact any, make a nice knot and walk away twirling the bag as they go. And the dog must think he's king of the world. He's 'got a guy' picking up his shit for him.

What a boon for the plastic bag industry. Some reports indicate that 69 million households have a pet dog and there are about 90 million pet dogs in the U.S.  Let's see, 90,000,000 times twice a day, times 365… that's 65,700,000,000 (65 billion 700 million) plastic bags needed every year for dog crap. Of course, that calculation assumes everyone uses these bags and doesn't just carry one for show. Another thought, assuming these bags are 12 inches long, if they were placed end to end, they would reach around the earth 500 times.

One last situation. Some dog people walk their dogs, meet other people with dogs, stop and have a nice conversation. Others may join and pretty soon dog walking can become a popular social outing. Here's the problem, the dog walkers only know the names of the other dogs, not the other dog owners' names. Subsequent conversations between them can go like this:

"I hear Fluffy's parents are getting a divorce."
"Did you hear Digger's dad passed away?"
"Molly's mom got a new car."

You see? I rest my case.
I need to quickly call-off this candid commentary on the canine cosmos. (Oh, I do love alliteration!)

**Regulations Regarding Dogs**

Most communities have regulations regarding dogs. Licenses are required ($$$), rabies shots ($$$), number and type of dogs, dog behavior, etc. It's another set of reasons not to have a dog.

# AKC ($$$$$)

This is an organization which, among many other things, registers purebred dogs. You know, pure breeds with ridiculously long names like Benjamin Lancelot Mullington VonQuay IV…we call him Zeke.

The AKC categorizes dog breeds into 7 Groups:

**Sporting Group**

Bred to assist hunters in the capture and retrieval of feathered game. The Labrador Retriever, German Shorthaired Pointer and Cocker Spaniel are among those in this group. My advice, don't let them near the badminton court.

**Hound Group**

Bred to pursue warm-blooded quarry, this group includes Bloodhound, Dachshund, and Greyhound. Obviously, any breed with 'hound' or 'hund' in the name. Even I can understand this group.

**Working Group**

Bred to assist humans by pulling sleds or carts, guarding flocks and homes and protecting families. The Boxer, Great Dane and Rottweiler are in this group. Basically, you only see the back end of these.

**Terrier Group**

Bred to go underground in pursuit of rodents and other vermin. These include Bull Terrier, Scottish Terrier and Welsh Terrier. Here again, probably any breed with 'Terrier' in the name. "Hey Cooper, go fetch us a weasel for dinner!"

## Toy Group

Bred to fit comfortably in the lap of their adoring owners, the Chihuahua, Pug and Shih Tzu are in the Toy group. What size lap is used as the standard? John Candy or Mini-Me? Actually, a toy dog is any that you can walk using dental floss as a leash.

## Non-Sporting Group

Bred to have four legs and wet noses, Bulldog, Dalmatian and Poodle are in this group. Probably should have called this group 'Miscellaneous.' Furthermore, doesn't Non-Sporting Group also include any breeds that aren't 'Sporting,' such as Terrier, Toy, Working, Hound and Herding?

## Herding Group

Bred to move livestock, including sheep, cattle and reindeer—the Border Collie, German Shepherd and Corgi are good examples. Santa Claus probably has a dog in this group.

# Beware of This Dangerous Trio

Most people know many famous trios. Just to hazard a guess, I reckon the following are generally well-known.

- Lions and Tigers and Bears (Oh My!)
- Snap, Crackle and Pop
- The Good, The Bad and The Ugly
- Stop, Drop and Roll
- Bacon, Lettuce and Tomato
- Moe, Larry and Curly
- Huey, Dewey and Louie

and

- Chico, Harpo and Groucho

Are you with me now?

Seriously, dog owners need to be aware of a very ominous, dangerous and ubiquitous trio, **Worms, Fleas and Ticks**.

Worms are internal parasites and fleas and ticks external. These parasites can infect your dog and might be passed on to you. Treatments are available as well as preventive measures. ($$$)

Do you itch, feel your intestines crawling, comb your hair hourly, or do full body checks daily? You probably have 'Doggie Trio Syndrome.' Don't worry, very easily treated. Give little Dumpling to a cousin you don't care for.

# Dog Names

Every dog needs a name. Otherwise, how would you call it for dinner or chastise it? If there were no name, what would every stranger ask about your dog, other than "How old is she?"

Here's the dog owner meets stranger scenario "Oh how cute, what's her name? Awwwww, how old is she?" Every dog owner should just wear a t-shirt that says 'Lucy, 17 months' to save time in the doggie-centric tête-à-tête.

For me, when I see a person with a dog, I don't want to know its name. I don't want to know how old it is. I don't say anything. I just think, "God, I'm glad I don't have to feed that thing," or "Imagine the size of his turds," or "Egad, that lady and her dog have matching sweaters," or "Yikes, what's he licking now?" (I mean the dog.)

Most of us know many famous dog names, real, fictitious or cartoon. Snoopy, Benji, Bullet, Yukon King, Old Yeller, Daisy, Petey, Beethoven, Sandy, Lady and the Tramp, Clifford, Balto, Bo, Fly, Buddy, Einstein, Fala, Scooby Doo, Pluto, Toto, Rin Tin Tin, Hooch, Eddie, Odie, Rex the Wonder Dog and so on.

I like the fictitious and cartoon dogs best. No ($$$), No (***)

I have categorized dog names into three groups.

**Typical or Traditional Names**
(These make *some* sense)

Fido, Spot, Rex, Buddy, Bandit, Old Blue, King, Joy, Sparky, Lady, Pepper, Hunter, Lancer, Rover.

**People Names**
(These make *no* sense)

George, Fred, Rosie, Oscar, Winston, Leo, Chloe, Samantha, Abby.

**Weird Names**
(What the ####?)

Jayla, Booger, Aja, Zyla, Yeti, Ayla.

**However, If I Named the Dogs**

How about—Drools, Fartzy, Sheds, Scoots, Lix, Humpz?

**Helpful Hint:** It is very easy to avoid the frustration of trying to find the best, most appropriate name for your new dog—just don't get one!

# Kenneling Your Dog

Persons who are unable to care for their dog(s) for any length of time have the option to put them in a kennel. You know, a money-making business catering to people who shouldn't have dogs ($$$). This is effectively jail for dogs. I don't think dogs like being placed in the 'Slammer.'

Dogs, like your Pomeranian, can pick up many diseases from other dogs when kenneled. One is 'kennel cough.' It can be bacterial or viral and causes little Snookers to cough, retch, sneeze, snort, gag or vomit, and maybe get a fever.

This can be treated with antibiotics ($$$) or prevented by vaccinating ($$$). Just another fun fact in the world of canine ownership.

# Spaying/Neutering Dogs

Spaying is the term used to describe the surgical procedure ($$$) for female dogs in which the ovaries and/or uterus are removed to sterilize her. Dog licenses may be less expensive after this procedure.

Neutering is the term used to describe the surgical procedure ($$$) for male dogs in which both testi.....never mind, can't go on, just pay the higher license fee.

# Dog Years

Actually, there is no such thing as a dog year. Stay with me now. If you own a dog (fingers crossed you don't!) and keep it for a year, you are one year older, and the dog is one year older. Capeesh?

Don't get caught up in the 'Rule of Paw' that states that one dog year is equal to 7 human years. That is used by dog owners to soften the blow that dogs' life spans are short.

Dog minutes, on the other hand, are real. When I spend 10 minutes in the company of some dogs, it seems like 10 months. So, a minute with a dog is equal to a human month. "I said SOME dogs!" Relax, already!

# Dog Breeds

How many dog breeds are there? Apparently TNTC. (Bacteriologists know this as Too Numerous To Count.)

The AKC lists about 200 different breeds while the FCI (Fédération Cynologique Internationale) lists about 360. Nice correlation there, I reckon there's a little friction between the USA and 'Over Yonder' about this discrepancy. It seems a little cattywampus to me. (Or is it doggywompus?)

A comment about dog breeds. What makes a pure breed? All current purebreds were created by mating one kind of dog with another. That first litter was the original pure breed of that ilk. Why aren't other mutts or mongrels pure examples of a new breed?

And another thing. When is this cross breeding going to stop? There are hundreds if not thousands of cross breed dogs. This could go on to infinity…and beyond.

Here are a few recognized, hybrid or designer dogs. (Read: mutts.)

- Labradoodle (Labrador Retriever-Poodle mix)
- Goldendoodle (Golden Retriever-Poodle mix)
- Morkie (Maltese-Yorkshire Terrier mix)
- Dalmadoodle (Dalmatian-Poodle mix)
- Pomsky (Pomeranian-Siberian Husky mix)
- Puggle (Pug-Beagle mix)
- Cockapoo (Cocker Spaniel-Poodle mix)
- Bernedoodle (Bernese Mountain Dog-Poodle mix)
- Chiweenie (Chihuahua-Dachshund mix)
- Westiepoo (West Highland White Terrier-Poodle mix)
- Schnoodle (Miniature Schnauzer-Miniature Poodle mix)
- Newfiepoo (Newfoundland-Poodle mix)
- Goldador (Golden Retriever-Labrador Retriever mix)

(Gotta quit now, this could go on forever.)

You see how out of control this has gotten? Could those names get any worse? Chiweenie?

Moving on...
The following pages contain a listing of 50 dog breeds and their main characteristics, with illustrations. You may wonder why 50 dog breeds? Well, the AKC lists about 200 breeds, but I thought that would be too many. Fifty is a nice number. I chose 50 for the following reasons:

1. The US has 50 States.
2. Paul Simon sang about *50 Ways to Leave Your Lover*.
3. NBAer David Robinson (the Admiral) wore number 50.
4. Fifty years is the Golden wedding Anniversary.
5. $3^2 + 4^2 + 5^2 = 50$.
6. 50 is the atomic number for Tin (Symbol Sn, Latin: stannum.)
7. My IQ typically hovers around 50.

For each breed of dog listed we offer:

1. The Name of the Breed.
2. The Scientific, Taxonomic Name for the Breed. (Genus species).
3. Points to Consider.
4. Famous Dogs of that Breed.
5. Verdict as to whether I recommend one should consider this breed for a pet.
6. An illustration of the dog breed for your enjoyment.

(A few are illustrated in the style of a famous artist. Can you find Vincent Van Gogh, Edvard Munch and Andy Warhol?)

Good reading!

# Making the Case (or Not) for 50 Breeds of Dogs

# Akita

## *(Chopstickae nippon)*

**Points To Consider**

The Akita is a Japanese dog. We already have Honda®, Toyota®, Canon®, Nintendo®, Sony®, etc. Do we really need an Akita?

They were used by the Samurai for bear hunting. Akitas are not tolerant of dogs of the same sex, are not well-suited for off-leash dog parks and are heavy shedders. Need I go on?

In 1931, the Akita was officially declared a Japanese natural monument. (I wonder how Mount Fuji felt about that?)

These 'heavy shedders' can go heavier than normal twice a year. These biannual events are referred to as 'blowing out the coat.' (Sounds dangerous. Are explosives used?) So, they either shed a lot or a hell of a lot. No black slacks for you!

They are very picky eaters. Not about what they eat, but about utensils. They will only eat with chopsticks. Be ready for a lot of clean up. Having no opposable thumb can make this quite a mess.

**Famous Akitas**

Helen Keller introduced the first Akitas to the U.S. in 1937. She had received 'Kamikaze-go' and 'Kenzan-go' as gifts from Mr. Ogasawara of Japan. (We all know of Helen, but who in Izanami's name is Ogasawara?)

**Verdict**

I checked on this breed,
Looking for good, but alas,
Only negative.

*(Written as a haiku, Japanese short form poetry.)*

akita

# Basset Hound

## (Leatherus humongus)

**Points To Consider**

Basset Hounds are large, short, solid and long with curved tails. Bred to hunt hare (and probably shed it.) The name Basset is derived from the French words 'bas' (low) and 'et', together meaning rather low.

Their colors can be lemon and white, white and chocolate, black and brown, tricolor, black and white, or red and white. What is this, a mixed drink/wine offering?

Their hanging skin structure causes the face to have a sad look. The very large ears (referred to as 'leathers') must be cleaned frequently, inside and out, to prevent infection from ear mites. Their lungs are strong and they can howl loudly. They are prone to yeast infections in the folds around the mouth where drool can collect. Several reasons to give one paws. Are you thinking, "probably not going to do a lot of hare hunting anyway?"

**Famous Basset Hounds**

- In 1956, Elvis sang *Hound Dog* on TV to a disinterested Basset Hound.
- A Basset Hound graced the cover of Time® magazine February 27,1928.
- The lonely Maytag® repairman has one.
- But the best is the mascot for Hush Puppies® Shoes who appears in many ads.

**Verdict**

'Rather low' opinion of this guy, even on a 'starry night.'

*(Illustration à la Vincent Van Gogh)*

Basset
Hound

# Beagle

## *(Hundus contrabandusdetectus)*

**Points To Consider**

The Beagle is a breed of small scent hound which was developed in Great Britain primarily for hunting hare, known as 'beagling.' Many famous public schools and universities had packs of Beagles. (Huh?) Makes sense, I guess. The breed has always been characterized by the phrase, "Barks Well With Others."

The Beagle is known for two main characteristics:

(1) They have an excellent sense of smell and can detect illegal substances as well as food or game.

(2) They can fly a Sopwith Camel airplane and engage in dogfights against enemy pilots, such as the Red Baron.

**Famous Beagles**

- That one cartoon dog who has a yellow bird for a friend. His owner is a lovable loser.
- U.S. President Lyndon Johnson's Beagle, strangely enough named 'Him.' The one he picked up by the ears on the White House lawn, much to many-a-dog lovers' chagrin.

**Verdict**

Houston, we have a problem. This Beagle hasn't landed. You shouldn't land one either.

Beagle

# Bichon Frise

## *(Canis blanca)*

### Points To Consider

Bichon Frise is French for curly haired dog. Imagine a white Oscar the Grouch®. They are a small breed weighing 10-20 pounds and 9-10 inches high at the withers. (The withers is a point on the dog's back which you can't find in all that curly-hair, so measure from wherever you please.)

The AKC states that these dogs are merry and curious. Because of this, they have been much travelled and were actually used as barter by Italian sailors as they moved about long ago. I hope they received some good rum in exchange for these little, curious, oversized hairballs. (Rum, the other 'Man's Best Friend.')

The AKC states that the standard coat color is pure white. Apricot, grey and brown are not recognized. Little known fact—this gave rise to that old derisive expression, "You're as relevant as a brown Bichon!"

### Famous Bichon Frises

None appearing. Some can be seen on social media if you're bored enough to look. Let's face it, you have too much time on your hands if you are reading blogs from a dog! Stop and do something productive. (Admonishing for a friend.)

### Verdict

No, especially if you already have a dust mop.

Bichon Frise

# Black and Tan Coonhound

## *(Canis guinness)*

### Points To Consider

The Black and Tan Coonhound is a hunting dog that runs down its game by scent and is used primarily for hunting raccoons. (What is the daily bag limit for raccoons in your state? Don't know? Odds are you're not a raccoon hunter.)

A coonhound will wander off if it catches a scent. Just try to keep one with you at a farmer's market. Its bark is loud and baying. Your neighbors will love you.

Have you found your reason to discount this breed yet? I could go on—double dog dare me!

### Famous Black and Tan Coonhounds

George Washington and Thomas Jefferson had Black and Tan Coonhounds. Apparently, raccoon hunting didn't interest any other U.S. President. And why didn't John Adams have one to complete the trifecta?

Another famous one is the beer mixture that English call Black and Tan, a mix of a stout beer and a pale ale, like, Guinness Stout® and Bass Pale Ale®. Now that's a famous Black and Tan. Cheers, chaps!

### Verdict

No, this dog just won't hunt. But a thumbs up on the beer!

Black and Tan
Coonhound
Dog
beer

# Bloodhound

## *(Hundus hemoglobinae)*

### Points To Consider

Originally bred for hunting and tracking people. Today, Bloodhound identification of a suspect can help police with inquiries. Evidence of identification is accepted in some courts.

They weigh 80-160 lbs and are 23-27 inches tall at the withers. Withers? I thought he sang *Ain't No Sunshine*.

Anyway, they're big. And they smell good or is it smell well? God's truth, I've never smelled one.

Unfortunately, Bloodhounds suffer an unusually high rate of gastric dilation volvulus (Bloat.) Isn't that special?

They are one of the shortest-lived breeds with a lifespan of about 6.75 years. (That's six and three quarters for you non-math people or the square root of 45.5625 for you math nerds.) That'll surely screw up the 'dog years' calculation.

### Famous Bloodhounds

McGruff, the crime dog. (That's crime, not grime, but could go either way). Never noticed how bloated he is.

### Verdict

Who wants bloated dog who will die young, anyway?

your witness
Bloodhound

# Boxer

## *(Cassius clae)*

### Points To Consider

Boxer sounds a little intimidating to me. There are three types of Boxers: American Boxer, German Boxer and English Boxer.

Boxers have very strong jaws and a powerful bite, ideal for holding on to large prey. (Caution: Don't let Aunt Sharon pet one if she has recently been making liver sausage sandwiches! That might leave a mark.)

One source surmised that Boxers got their name because they like to play by standing on their hind legs and 'boxing' with their front paws. Not so cute to Grandma Donna, with a bad hip, carrying a full tray of champagne flutes.

The recognized colors of a Boxer are 'fawn' and 'brindle.' Are these even colors? Would we sing "Brindle suede shoes"? or "Little fawn Corvette"? I didn't think so.

### Famous Boxers

***American:*** Sugar Ray Leonard
***German:*** Max Schmeling
***English:*** Tyson Fury

### Verdict

Nope, I give this breed a KO.

(Author's Note: Unfortunately, Emily's illustration for this dog was misplaced. Press time was imminent, so I asked my wife to quickly do a replacement drawing. She's not an artist, but I give her credit for a good effort. Mea culpa.)

BOXER
(See note)

# Bulldog

## *(Mandibularus capacious)*

**Points To Consider**

The Bulldog was bred in England to look like Winston Churchill. How they knew in the 1600s what Churchill would look like in the 1940s is a doggone mystery to this day. They are a breed of the mastiff type, medium-sized, muscular, and weigh 40-55 pounds. (That's pound Avoirdupois Weight, not the Pound Sterling, there's a ton of difference.)

They have a flat face, protruding lower jaw, and wide head and shoulders. They were bred as companion dogs from the Old English Bulldog. This now extinct breed was used for bull-baiting, which gave the name to the breed. Bull-baiting was a blood sport pitting a tethered bull against several dogs. The aim was to attack and subdue the bull by biting and holding onto its nose or neck, which often resulted in the death of the bull. Many dogs were maimed or killed as well. Spectators would bet on the outcome. (Not for me, I'd prefer a nice vigorous game of lawn bowling—rarely anyone dies.)

One report said the median age at death for a Bulldog is 6 years and 3 months. I wonder what the mean and mode ages were. (Asking for my nerd friend.) Anyway, they don't live very long. Most common cause of death is being gored by a tethered bull.

**Famous Bulldogs**

- The Mack® truck trademark hood ornament is a Bulldog.
- 'Uga', the mascot of the University of Georgia athletic teams. Goooooo DAWGS, Sic 'em! Woof! Woof! Woof! Woof! Woof!

**Verdict**

No, and I mean it. No Bull.

Bulldog

# Cairn Terrier

## *(Jayhawkus dorothea)*

**Points To Consider**

The Cairn Terrier breed originated in the Scottish Highlands and is recognized as one of the earliest working dogs.

The name Cairn Terrier was a compromise since Short-haired Skye Terrier was not accepted by the Kennel Club. (How they then named it after a man-made pile of stones is anybody's guess. Probably a suggestion from a real rock hound.)

Brindled (whatever that is) Cairn Terriers can gradually change color throughout their lifetimes. A brindled Cairn can become more black or silver as it ages. (Changing to black is remarkable but don't all of us get more silver as we age?)

Just because Toto was a Cairn Terrier doesn't mean you should have one as a pet. They are known to jump out of bicycle baskets and pull curtains open!

**Famous Cairn Terriers**

That little crapper in *The Wizard of Oz*.

(Fun Fact: Toto was played by a Cairn Terrier named Terry. Terry's owner was paid $125 per week during filming but the Munchkins were each paid a measly $50-$100 per week.)

**Verdict**

The Tin Man and I don't have the heart to recommend one.

Cairn Terrier

# Chihuahua

## *(Perro diminutia)*

**Points To Consider**

The Chihuahua is a Mexican breed of dog and is usually kept as a companion. Awww, sounds like 'Amor de cachorros' to me. That's 'puppy love,' comprende?

The Chihuahua is considered the smallest breed in the world. That's not a great reason to help you determine which dog to bring home. By the way, why is there a second 'hua' in the name, why repeat it? Wouldn't Chihua have been enough?

Spanish for Chihuahua is Chihuahueño. Be sure to enunciate well when ordering chile relleno at a restaurant, you could mistakenly be served a small dog.

Current breed standards include an apple-head or apple-dome skull formation! They must mean crab apples, Granny Smiths are way too big.

Some breeders try to breed very small or 'teacup' Chihuahuas.
"Would you like a Chihuahua with your scone, señora?"

**Famous Chihuahuas**

There is scant information about any 'famous' examples of these wee creatures. A Google search for famous chihuahuas yielded a blank page. No results at all in 7,655.4 seconds.

Oh, wait. One just popped up. It's Gidget, the Taco Bell® mascot who used to say "¡Yo quiero Taco Bell!"

**Verdict**

No Way José.

Chihuahua

# Chow Chow

## *(Chopchop sueysuey)*

**Points To Consider**

The Chow Chow originated in China China. The breed is unique because of its purple/black tongue tongue (Lingua purpura.) The breed is also known for its very dense coat coat (Tunica densissima) and the fur is particularly thick around the neck neck. They should be brushed four times a week week, even more in shedding season season. (***) (***)

They are resistant to training—aggressive, stubborn and can raise the cost ($$$) of homeowner's insurance because they are high risk risk.

How many more reasons do you need to pass on this breed breed?

Oh, and their food is expensive ($$$), as they need extra MSG on their Gravy Train® Train.

**Famous Chow Chows**

None None. But there have been famous owners including Georgia O'Keefe, Sigmund Freud, Martha Stewart, Calvin Coolidge, Elvis Presley, Janet Jackson, and Walt Disney Disney.

**Verdict**

No No

Not your chow, Chow Chow
Lady
Chow Chow

The Cocker Spaniel
*slurp*

# Cocker Spaniel

*(Uarso beautifulus)*

## Points To Consider

Cocker Spaniels were originally bred as hunting dogs in the UK, with the term 'cocker' deriving from their use to hunt the Eurasian woodcock. Need a lot of them to feed a family as woodcocks are only 'appetizer' size.

The dog Obo II is considered to be the progenitor of the Cocker Spaniel and is claimed to be the sire or grandsire of nearly every prize winning Cocker in America. Additionally, he was the sire of the double reed woodwind instrument used to tune orchestras.

Talk about a loser breed. It was the most popular breed in the U.S. from 1936 to 1952. By 2009 it had fallen to 13th. Now ranks 23rd in popularity. Rodney Dangerfield probably had one.

## Famous Cocker Spaniels

Lady from the animated movie *Lady and the Tramp*. The famous kiss with Tramp as they each ate on opposite ends of a strand of spaghetti is a classic. But let's talk about Tramp. He's obviously not a purebred as there is no mention of his breed. Apparently his dam was out putting on the dog quite often with the studs. One might consider she was the 'Tramp.'

## Verdict

No, unless you have a significant woodcock problem.

# Collie

## *(Lassius comehomus)*

**Points To Consider**

The Collie originated in Scotland and Northern England where it was used for herding cattle, sheep and other livestock. The name may have been derived from the Scots word for 'coal' or 'coolly.'

There are Border Collies, Bearded Collies, Rough Collies and Smooth Collies. As the Scots say, "Whae the Haol Do Wee Nee So Mae?"

The Border Collie is the smartest dog according to Coren. In the finals of the intelligence competition, he amazed the judges by answering the following questions quickly and correctly.

1. What is the topmost part of a house called?
2. In golf, what is the area outside the fairway?
3. How do we characterize sandpaper?

Lassie was a Rough Collie who was the renowned television and movie star. Fly was a Border Collie and had a successful role in the movie Babe.

People will try to tell you that Collies are herding dogs, but I bet Lassie and Fly never saw a sheep, let alone a flock of them. No doubt these two had huge egos and required expensive extra special treatment. Think gourmet dog food, pedicures, barking lessons, chauffeur, and lush accommodations ($$$).

**Famous Collies**

They're mentioned above, weren't you paying attention?

**Verdict**

No, but if you raise sheep, it could be a maybe.

I can't right now. I have a Mensa meeting.
Border Collie

# Dachshund

## *(Doggonus frankfurterae)*

**Points To Consider**

Yes, this is the famous 'Wiener Dog.' Why would you want a dog that looks like a wiener? A common litter size is 6 pups. But we all know the buns come in packages of 8! How hard is this? Is this 'new' math?

Dachshund is German for 'badger-dog' because they were bred to hunt badgers. I'd imagine the people from Wisconsin would have great aversion to this breed.

These puppies are looooong and their legs are short. Anything else? Oh yeah, this must be the dog talked about in the cowboy ballad, "Whoopee Ti Yi Yo, Get a long little doggie."

Someone famous once said that a Dachshund is "Half a dog high and a dog-and-a-half long." That person was me, but I was quoting someone else more clever.

**Famous Dachshunds**

- Lump, the pet of Pablo Picasso who was thought to have inspired some of his art.
- 'Slinky Dog' from the *Toy Story* movies.
- Ball Park®
- Hebrew National®

**Verdict**

Nein, no ~~soup~~ dog for you!

Dachshund

# Dalmatian

## *(Cruellus deVil)*

**Points To Consider**

You can spot these spotted dogs from far away. You'd be spot-on to think that spotting them in many different spots was easy.

They can be spotted at a firehouse, in a spot atop the Budweiser beer wagon, and many other well-known spots.

Dalmatians are named for Dalmatia, a historical region on the eastern shore of the Adriatic Sea in Croatia. It's a very nice spot. You should go there and see if you can spot any Dalmatians.

I've spotted a few health issues they can suffer from: Deafness, hip dysplasia, and hyperuricemia (high uric acid in urine, gout, kidney and bladder stones). Many dog days ahead if you own this breed.

**Famous Dalmatians**

- I believe I spotted 101 of them, in a movie or something. Anyway, they were spotlighted in it.
- Dalmatian wine is also very famous. Dalmatia is known for its red and white wines. Word to the wise—drink too much, you'll be sick as a dog and will need hair of the dog the next day.

**Verdict**

No. I'll go with spot remover on this one.

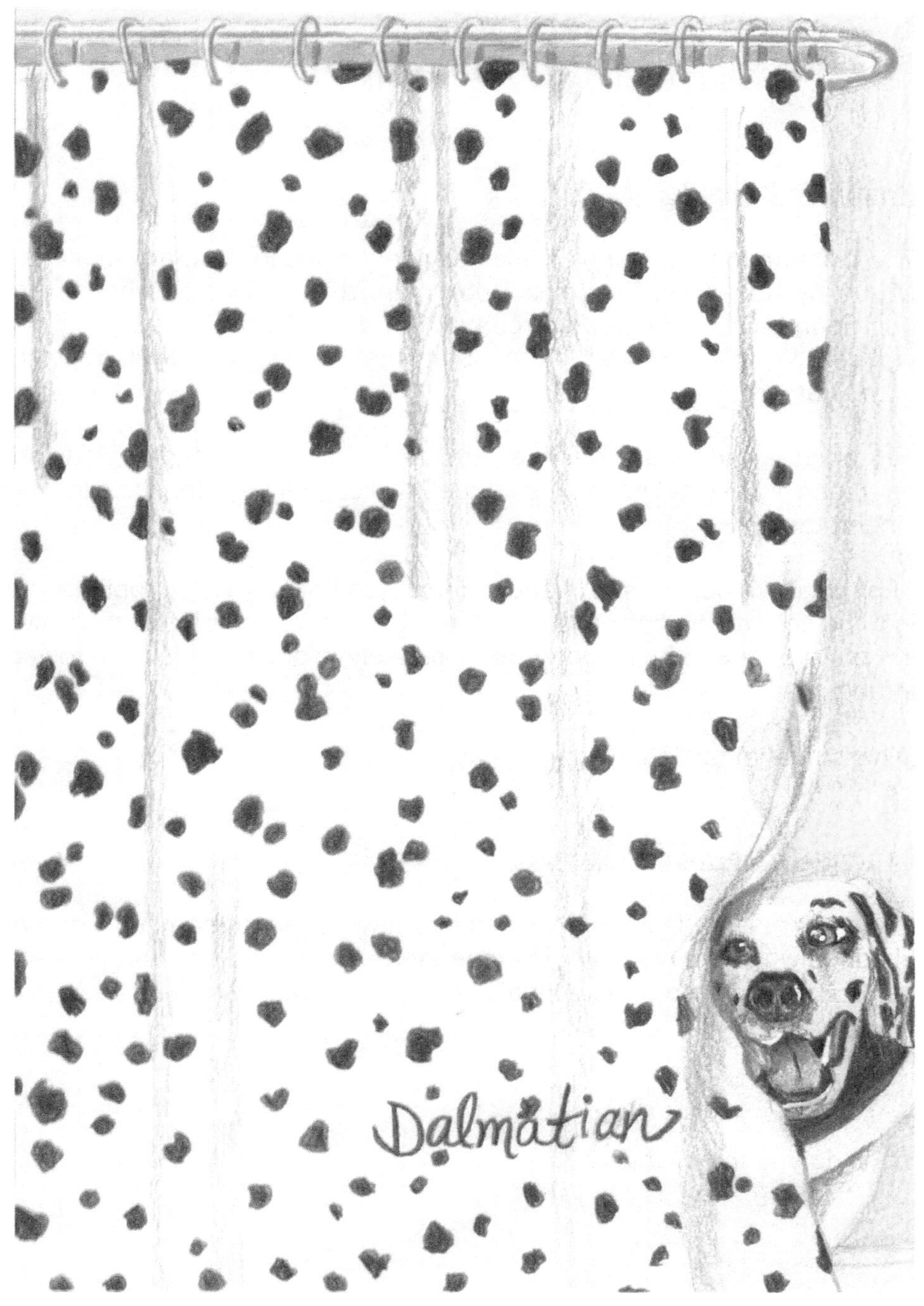
Dalmatian

# Doberman Pinscher

*(Attackus grrrrrr)*

**Points To Consider**

The Doberman Pinscher was originally developed in Germany in the late 1800s by Karl Friedrich Louis Doberman, a tax collector who ran the dog pound. OK, now you're probably wondering, can this story get any weirder? What's next, he fed them bratwurst and liverwurst with a pinsch of mustard?

Talk about a bad reputation. They are stereotyped as being ferocious and aggressive! Let's get several, shall we? All I can say is, "Thanks a lot Herr Doberman!"

They do have canine intelligence; being good at learning, problem-solving and communication. They can learn to respect and protect their owners but are ranked high in breeds more likely to show aggression toward strangers.

(That's a lot of talk about aggression!)

**Famous Doberman Pinschers**

Infamous maybe. Doberman Pinschers have been in many movies and almost always are portrayed as their stereotype indicates, dangerous to be around! For example, 'Alpha' in the movie *Up*.

**Verdict**

What do you think I think?

# Doberman Pinscher

# English Setter

## *(Limey birdoggus)*

**Points To Consider**

The English Setter is a gentle but strong-willed, mischievous, gun dog bred to hunt quail, pheasant and grouse. It has a mainly white coat with long silky fringes on the back of the legs, under the belly and on the tail. It can actually function as a roving dust mop around the flat, or like a bloody robot vacuum cleaner.

The base coat is white with differing coloured ticking; also called flecks or speckling. (Didn't you blokes ever consider it was just mud from the hunt?)

They are considered very intelligent but only ranked 37th in intelligence by Coren. They probably can't even calculate the area of a triangle. (That's 1/2 BxH for some of you, innit?)

Plus they need at least 2 hours of exercise per day. And no, you can't just do 14 hours on Sunday.

**Famous English Setters**

- Shadow Oak Bo, a two-time National Champion Bird Dog.
- Count Noble was popularly known as the '$10,000 hunting dog' and a 'national symbol of what was great in bird dogs.' After his death in 1891, his preserved body was displayed in the Carnegie Museum of Natural History in Pittsburgh, PA. (Creepy?)

**Verdict**

I say old chap, "Not on Your Nelly!"

English Setter

# Fox Terrier, Wirehaired

*(Steelwoolus coiffure)*

**Points To Consider**

The Wirehaired Terrier was developed in England by fox hunting enthusiasts. They were bred to hunt not only foxes but also badgers and boars. They have no more fear of cows or buses than they have of small prey. (So, take one along next time you go cow hunting on a bus.)

They have predominantly white coats with brown markings and usually a black saddle. (Must be a pretty small cowboy to ride these.)

They have a low threshold for boredom and require stimulation, exercise and near constant attention. (Sounds just like the kids these days.)

Often, Wirehaired Terriers are abandoned or surrendered for reasons like running away, chasing vehicles, and taunting and attacking other animals. (Step right up, we've got a blue light special on abandoned Wirehaireds today!)

Amazingly, as of 2019, the Wirehaired has the distinction of having more Best in Show titles at the Westminster Kennel Club Dog Show than any other breed.

**Famous Wirehaired Terriers**

Asta, the Wirehaired Terrier owned by Nick and Nora Charles of *The Thin Man* fame. If you don't know that, you don't do many crossword puzzles.

**Verdict**

The Westminster judging panel just sent a wire…No.

FOX
Terrier
I is the
foxiest.

# German Shepherd

## *(Mansbestus friendi)*

### Points To Consider

German Shepherds are considered dogkind's finest all-purpose worker. Bred in Germany (surprise, surprise) to be agile, muscular, courageous, intelligent, confident and have a tail. Other adjectives abound: Curious, stubborn, loyal, alert, confident, obedient, protective, watchful, courageous and brave.

Sounds like the perfect dog—if there were one.

German Shepherds have been used as police dogs, guard dogs and search/rescue dogs. Also notable is their use as guide dogs. (Wow, I just can't seem to find anything to comment on negatively here.)

Can be picky eaters. They don't care for Alpo® or Iams®, but prefer thüringer wurst, braunschweiger, wienerschnitzel and schweinshaxe. Verstehen sie?

### Famous German Shepherds

Oh, many years ago two German Shepherds were famous as movie stars. Strongheart made movies in the 1920s followed by Rin Tin Tin (plus Rin Tin Tin Jr. and Rin Tin Tin III) who made movies from the 1920s to the 1940s. Both dogs have stars on the Hollywood Walk of Fame. Several others have made movies since.

The most famous in my opinion are the German Shepherds that are medal recipients for assisting mankind with police work, search and rescue work, military work and guard dog work. Many lives are saved by these guys. Also, a shout out to the guide dogs for their compassionate role.

### Verdict

These guys are close, but nein zigarre.

German
Shepherd

# Golden Retriever

## *(Fetchum incessantus)*

### Points To Consider

This is a Scottish breed of fetching dog. Since the 1940s, this breed has been very popular and is one of the most recognized and frequently registered breeds in the Western world. They make excellent pets and family dogs, are easy to train and are keen to please their master. (That's keen as in 'eager' not ken like the Scottish 'recognize' or 'understand.') Goldens are generally calm and biddable. (Biddable? Kinda like a 13 point bridge hand, d'ye ken?)

They aren't strong swimmers as the long coat causes them to sit low in the water. So let them play in the sprinkler but keep them out of the hot tub, for more reasons than their aquatic incompetence. The Golden owner will spend a lot of time grooming. Cleaning dirt and picking out burrs (***) from the coat is time consuming and prevents the owner from participating in many other things, such as having a life!

Goldens have a strong instinct to retrieve and often present their owners with toys or balls to throw. This may be okay if you don't mind a slimy, sodden plush toy at your feet at all times.

### Famous Golden Retrievers

- Liberty, President Gerald R. Ford's Golden.
- Mayor Max, elected to be mayor of Idyllwild, CA in June 2012. Thus began a series of events leading to several succeeding Golden Retrievers being elected mayor of this unincorporated community.

### Verdict

Let me 'retrieve' my recommendation…No.

Golden
Retriever

# Great Dane

## *(Copenhagenus abundato)*

**Points To Consider**

So, I looked up Great Dane and expected to find stories about Niels Bohr, Viggo Mortensen, Hans Christian Anderson, Caroline Wozniacki, Soren Kierkegaard, and Victor Borge, but no! Apparently, it's a dog breed.

I found that it is one of the largest-sized dog breeds on the planet. Great Danes hold the world record for 'the largest dog ever.' These guys are HUGE! They will fit through a doorway side-to-side, but maybe not top-to-bottom. May be OK in a house with ten-foot ceilings. Remember large dog means large 'everything'—think about it.

Due to its size, it has been dubbed the 'Apollo of Dogs.' (How anyone ever thought to compare them to a music theater in Harlem, I'll never understand.)

**Famous Great Danes**

- Marmaduke®, classic cartoon Great Dane.
- Astro®, the Jetsons' Great Dane of TV cartoon fame… from the future.
- Scooby Doo®, the Saturday morning cartoon Great Dane.

(Do you see a pattern here? All cartoon dogs! But that's OK by me since they don't shed, eat, pee, crap (***) or even come off the pages or out of the TV screen.)

**Verdict**

No.

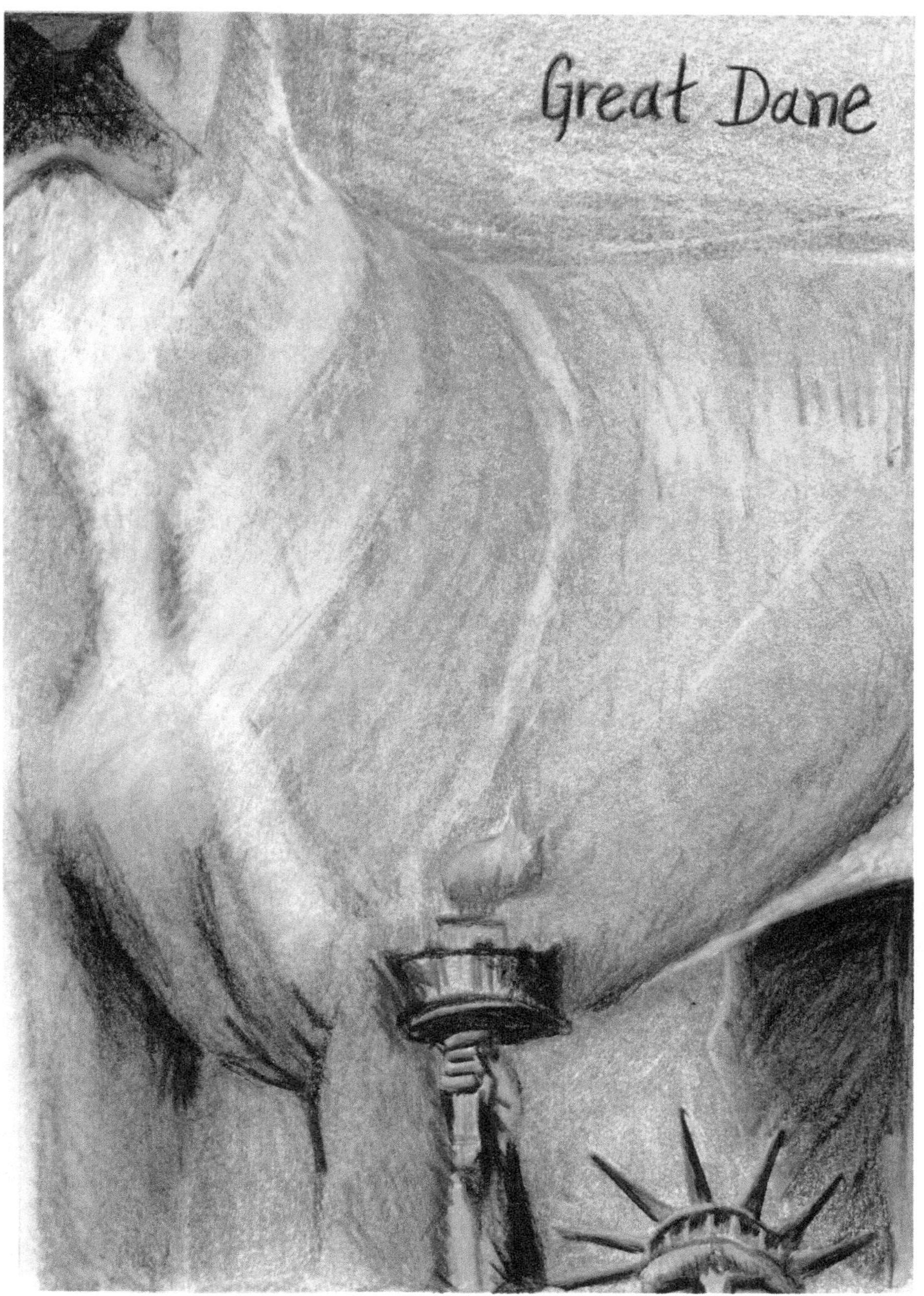
Great Dane

# Great Pyrenees

## *(Avalanchum blanco)*

### Points To Consider

The Great Pyrenees is a breed of livestock guardian dog from France, more particularly the French Alps and Pyrenees Mountains. These mountains straddle the border of France and Spain. (Thus ends your geography lesson for today.)

The name Great Pyrenees is used only in the U.S. In France, the breed is known as the Pyrenean Mountain Dog or the Patou. Do the French have to have a different word for everything? How do you pronounce Patou anyway? You probably don't pronounce some of the letters typical of most French words. C'est tellement frustrant!

If you like white, this is the dog for you. There will be white hair EVERYWHERE. I suggest you invest in lots of lint rollers before you get one of these. (I think 3M Scotch-Brite® has a new 144 pack.)

This is *another* sheepherding dog. Sometimes I think there are more sheepherding dogs than there are sheep. And when did we stop sheepherding and start putting coats on the dogs and taking them on a leash to arts and crafts shows?

### Famous Great Pyrenees

Don't know of any famous ones, but I heard there was a nice one in Renner, South Dakota.

### Verdict

No, being French they go oui oui all the time, and other faux paws.

Great Pyrenees
France↓
Spain

# Greyhound

## *(Drabus motorcoachus)*

**Points To Consider**

The Greyhound is a sighthound which means they can't smell well (and they don't smell good either.) They were bred for coursing. You know coursing, don't you? It's running down prey over long distances, like coast to coast. Probably what makes them OK at racing.

Greyhounds are tall, muscular, smooth-coated, S-shaped (What?) with a long tail and tough feet. There are about 30 recognized colors of greyhounds, or could you say about '30 Shades of Grey?'

They are known to take larger groups of people on sightseeing trips, usually with expert narration...Whoops, senior moment, I mixed up my reference material a little.

Adopting retired racing Greyhounds has become de rigueur and has increased the breed's popularity as pets. Makes no sense to me, there are not a lot of coursing opportunities around the house and yard! Don't let your greyhound out when Great Aunt Kyra is doing her senior yoga on the patio, she's not that fast!

**Famous Greyhounds**

Famous greyhound owners include: Cleopatra, Christopher Columbus, Babe Ruth, General George Custer, Al Capone, Brad Pitt, Frank Sinatra, Betty White, Queen Victoria, and King Henry VIII. Or maybe those were there most recent winners of the English Greyhound Derby. Whichever you think is funnier.

**Verdict**

No—Prone to chase those artificial rabbits you have laying around.

Greyhound

# Irish Setter

## *(Saintpatti relaxum)*

**Points To Consider**

I always get setter and sitter mixed up. An Irish sitter could be Bono in a Barcalounger, or Liam Neeson watching the neighbor's twin boys. But this one is an Irish '*Setter.*'

Apparently, the Irish Setter is breed of gundog and family dog. Gundog? (A dog trained to work alongside a loud firearm while hunting or retrieving game.)

They have long red hair which requires frequent brushing to keep it mat-free.

So, you can shoot your gun when grooming an Irish Setter with a dead partridge in its mouth and he won't flinch. Good to know.

Ireland's national bus and coach operator, Bus Eireann®, uses the Irish Setter as its corporate logo. (Take that, Greyhound® Lines!)

**Famous Irish Setters**

Kathleen O'Flaherty, the MVP of the University of Dublin's women's volleyball team. (Just kidding, I made that up.) But a setter is a very famous position in the sport of volleyball.

**Verdict**

Nil, this breed just doesn't set well with me.

Irish
Setter

# Labrador Retriever

*(Tennisballus bringbackus)*

## Points To Consider

The Labrador Retriever was developed in the UK from fishing dogs imported from Newfoundland. They are among the most commonly kept dogs in the Western world.

Dog experts describe these as 'high-spirited' which is just a shameless euphemism for hyperactive buggers. These tireless, slobbery, devils with a halo, will relentlessly fetch you a tennis ball to throw until you require Tommy John surgery. So, if you enjoy a very gross game of fetch, this could be the dog for you (if I were inclined to recommend one.)

Oh, and they come in black, yellow and chocolate colors. Chocolate is apparently another shameless euphemism for 'liver-colored.'

(How many times is he going to use 'shameless euphemism'? Wondering for a friend.)

## Famous Labrador Retrievers

Old Yeller. Whoops, he was a Yellow Labrador/Mastiff mix. Never mind.

Many Labrador Retrievers are famous for having excelled at search and rescue, military gallantry, explosives detection and devotion to duty. Nice.

## Verdict

No. No one has enough tennis balls, not even Wilson® or Dunlop® or Penn® or Prince® or Slazenger®.

Labrador Retriever

# Lhasa Apso

## *(Everest climerus)*

**Points To Consider**

This breed originated in Tibet a very long time ago. I found reference to 800 B.C. and to 800 A.D. Someone needs a better editor, that's 16 centuries difference. Either way, it's a long time ago. The breed has traditionally been used as an interior sentinel. (That's just a nice way of saying, "He barks like hell at the sound of the doorbell.")

There is debate over the exact origin of the name. Lhasa is obviously the capital city of Tibet. Apso may be the anglicized form of the Tibetan word for 'goatee' or 'billy goat' or 'bark guard.' It seems no one is really sherpa about this.

If you think the origin of the name is confusing, try classifying it into a breed group. The AKC originally put it in the Terrier Group, then transferred it to the Non-Sporting Group. In the U.K. they are placed in the Utility Group.

To meet the AKC standard, the coat should flow to the floor. I believe Swiffer® might be a good name for one but I'm not suggesting you get one, so, never mind.

**Famous Lhasa Apsos**

As with many of these kinds of dogs, there are no famous ones, only famous owners. Elizabeth Taylor, Liberace, Kurt Vonnegut, Ellen DeGeneres and Gwen Stefani to name a few. Alas, too bad they couldn't read this book first.

**Verdict**

Apso-lutely not!

Lhasa Apso
K2
Mt. Everest

# Maltese

## *(Milkshakus italiano)*

### Points To Consider

The Maltese is a dwarf canine from Italy. It competes in the Toy group. In recent competitions, it beat out Hula Hoop, Legos®, Barbie® and Rubik's Cube®. That was its quindici minuti of fame.

Very strict standards are set for this breed:

- A pure white coat is mandatory, although a pale ivory tinge is permitted. The ears should be hanging and the tail should curve over its back, however, a tail curved to one side is tolerated.
- Males need be 8-10 inches tall and bitches 8-9 inches tall.
- Maltese should weigh 7-9 pounds.
- The litter size is 1-3.
- Life span is 12-15 years.

Mamma Mia! Are you bored yet? How would one know if the tail is straight or curved in all that hair?

Maybe the best thing I can say about Maltese is that an owner can have a personalized license plate on his car that says, 'LVMYMLTZ.'

### Famous Maltese

Britney Spears and Meghan Markle have Maltese heritage. No Maltese dogs are famous enough to be cited here.

### Verdict

You're barking up the wrong olive tree if you think I recommend this one.

Maltese

# Newfoundland

## *(Colossuscanine eh)*

**Points To Consider**

Newfoundlands were bred in a newly found land, (Oh, now I get it) and were used as working dogs for fishermen in Newfoundland. (There it is again!)

They are known for their giant size, tremendous strength and intelligence. (Intelligence my foot, I bet one couldn't find Newfoundland on a map of eastern Canada.)

Egads, this breed is huge! Up to 250 pounds and it can eat right off the counter. Not the table, the counter! Speaking of eating, imagine the food processing machine he can be. ($$$) You're going to need some gigantic, strong, plastic 'lawn and garden size' bags to pick up after this guy. (***)

Apparently Newfies are very adept at water rescue, having a thick double coat, webbed paws (yikes) and dog paddle ability. However, you won't want him right back in the house after a episode in the ocean…think wet smelly black hair, salt water, possible seaweed. (***)

**Famous Newfoundlands**

'Nana' in *Peter Pan*, a novel and play by J.M. Barrie. But don't be fooled into thinking a dog can actually function as a nurse and nanny to a bunch of children, it is FICTION! And remember, she did allow the Darling's children to be snatched away to Neverland.

**Verdict**

No. How many water rescues are you anticipating, eh? I'd bet a Loonie or a Toonie not too many.

Which way to the water, eh?
CAN
Newfoundland

# Norwegian Elkhound

## *(Hundus lutefiskus)*

**Points To Consider**

The name Norwegian Elkhound is a mistranslation of the word 'elg' which means moose in Norwegian. And it is a Spitz breed not a Hound. So the name should have been Norwegian Moosespitz. Even after that snafu, it was named the National Dog of Norway. (The Swedish Toy Spaniel never had a shot at that honor.)

The Norwegian Elkhound is a hunter, guardian, herder and defender. When hunting, it tracks down and holds the moose at bay until the hunters arrive. (See, again, no elk in this story!)

The main problem with having one of these dogs is its Norwegian palate. It only eats:

- Lefse (Mashed Potato Flatbread)
- Fiskeboller i Hvit Saus (Fish Balls with Béchamel Sauce)
- Rømmegrøt (Sour Cream Porridge)
- Farikal (Mutton and Cabbage)
- Lutefisk (Dried or Salted Whitefish or Cod Cured in Lye)

All washed down with Aquavit.

Ja, you betcha, are you thinking the same as me? Not gonna to happen!

**Famous Norwegian Elkhounds**

"Weejie" pet dog of U.S. President Herbert Hoover.

Also, Edvard Munch, Roald Amundson, Henrik Ibsen, Anni-Frid Lyngstad, Erik the Red, Leif Eriksson and Roald Dahl. (Whoops, those are famous Norwegians. Never mind.)

**Verdict**

Uff Da, you can't a-fjord to have one.

Norwegian Elkhound

# Old English Sheepdog

## *(Fleecus prodigitus)*

**Points To Consider**

This archetypical 'Shaggy Dog' is an English (If that weren't obvious) herding dog. And it is the archetypical 'Hairball' also. They have been described as archetypical couch potatoes and may tend to 'herd' children by gently bumping them. (You know, like ten pins.) That's just not cricket!

How they see out from under all that hair is one of the *Seven Mysteries of the World*, or at least of Europe, or maybe of Great Britain, or maybe just of Hagley Road, Birmingham. And this isn't a 'Shaggy Dog' story, or is it? But seriously, can we get these guys some '*bangs*?'

These hair machines don't shed but DO require a thorough brushing at least once a week for 1-3 hours each time. (Blimey, that'll cut into your cocktail hour!) Some owners have been known to shave the Sheepdog's hair and spin it into yarn. (Cue the *Twilight Zone* music!)

Given all that hair however, they are the optimal choice for a 'three-dog night.'

**Famous Old English Sheepdogs**

- An Old English Sheepdog has been the brand mascot for Dulux® Paint.
- Martha, Paul McCartney's Sheepdog, was the inspiration for the Beatles song *Martha, My Dear*.

**Verdict**

Don't be a dunderhead, you'd be off your trolley to get one of these. Get a spot of tea instead.

Old English Sheepdog

# Pekingese

## *(Hirsutus greatwallus)*

**Points To Consider**

The Pekingese is a breed of toy dog originating in China having a flat face and large eyes. The very small Pekingese can be referred to as 'sleeves' since, in ancient times, emperors would carry the smallest in their sleeves. Hence, you could probably also carry one in your shirt pocket.

They must be kept indoors as their flattened faces and nasal structure can cause them to develop breathing problems, especially in hot climates. They are prone to Heatstroke, Congestive Heart Failure, Keratoconjunctivitis, Retinal Atrophy, and Glaucoma. One must remove foreign material from the eyes daily and clean the creases on the face to prevent sores.

Some Pekingese find stairs difficult and older ones may not be able to climb them at all. It is also necessary to maintain and groom the long fur at the 'rear end' as the area is prone to 'soiling.' So, this breed would suit you if you lived on first floor in a cold climate, had a groomer in the family, had a veterinary cardiologist and ophthalmologist on call, had reasonably sized shirt pockets, had a large supply of Q-tips®, and had rear end combs/brushes.

**Famous Pekingese**

The first Pekingese in Ireland was introduced by Dr. Heuston. He had established smallpox vaccination clinics in China and, in gratitude, the Chinese presented him with a pair. He named them Chang and Lady Li. Nice.

**Verdict**

No, if they can't climb stairs, how do you think they'd do on the Great Wall?

Pekingese

# Pembroke Welsh Corgi

## *(Abdomenus draggus)*

### Points To Consider

The Pembroke Welsh Corgi (PWC) is an achondroplastic (true dwarf) breed that originated in Pembroke, Wales. There is a similar breed, the Cardigan Welsh Corgi which hails from Cardigan, Wales (You know, Mr. Rogers' neighborhood.) But this story is about only PWCs.

Here's an interesting characteristic. Due to their herding and prey instincts, PWCs love to chase things and may nip at one's ankles as this is what they were bred to do with cattle. (So the Corgi is the origin of the term ankle-biter. Aha! Darn little pointy-eared short-legged dwarfs!)

It happens that PWCs are pretty good at flyball. Flyball is a sport in which dogs race over a line of hurdles to a box that releases a tennis ball to be caught when the dog presses a spring-loaded pad, and then back to their handler with the ball. I guess you CAN teach a SQUAT dog new tricks.

### Famous Pembroke Welsh Corgis

Corgis were the preferred breed of Queen Elizabeth II and she had more than thirty of them during her reign. The Queen's passion started when her father, King George VI, brought home 'Dookie.' The Queen ceased breeding Corgis around 2012 so as not to leave any behind after she died. Her last Corgi, 'Willow,' died in April 2018.

### Verdict

What part of ankle biting don't you understand? As they say in Wales, Nac.

Corgi
PRINCESS

# Pit Bull

## *(Axilla taurus)*

**Points To Consider**

(As a public service, and for the benefit of the younger readers, I'm going to start nearly every sentence with the word 'like.' As if that will make things clearer and more like, succinct.)

Like, what a wonderful (NOT) breed this is...Like, actually, this guy is super scary. Like, I literally died the first time I met one.

Like this breed is so totally horrifying. Like the AKC doesn't even recognize them as a breed. Like, some other dog groups do—whatever.

**Famous Pit Bulls**

None. Like, they're all like, *NOT* famous, fer shur.

**Verdict**

Like, NOOOOOO!

Pit Bull
Being this cute is ruff.

# Pointer

## *(Fingerus indexi)*

### "Points" To Consider

The Pointer was developed in England to find game for hunters. Sometimes called the English Pointer, this breed only points at prey but doesn't retrieve. Somewhat of a specialist there. He 'has people' to retrieve for him, who sometimes get into a kerfuffle over this.

Pointers can also locate game birds to be flushed for a falcon to dispatch. (Why do we waste euphemisms on falcons? Dispatch? They just kill them with their talons and hooked, toothed beak.)

Many people say that the Pointer is the ultimate pointing dog breed because of its sensitive nose, big stylish movements and flashy pointing stance. (Think: John Travolta as Tony Manero in *Saturday Night Fever*.)

### Famous Pointers

- Uncle Sam in the famous WWI Army recruiting poster "I Want You."
- Stevie, the mascot of the University of Wisconsin-Stevens Point. (The Pointers)
- Bonnie, Ruth, Anita and June, all early members of the Pointer Sisters singing group. They had many hits including *Jump (For My Love), Slow Hand* and *So Excited* in the 1980s. The group is still singing.

### Verdict

When the most famous ones are NOT dogs, what's the point?

# Pointer

# Pomeranian

## *(Cheerleadum shakerus)*

**Points To Consider**

This is a breed in the Toy Group named for Pomerania, a region in northwest Poland and northeast Germany on the Baltic Sea. But that isn't the origin of the breed. Make sense to you? They have an abundant textured coat with a highly plumed tail. Read: 'hair everywhere.' (***)

Pomeranians are one of the dog breeds having the smallest litter size with sources citing numbers between 1.9 and 2.7 puppies per litter. Be careful not to select the 0.9 pup or the 0.7 pup if considering this breed. You'll want a whole dog and will likely be charged for one anyway.

A common disorder in males is cryptorchidism, a condition in which one or both testicles do not descend into the scrotum. This is treated by surgical removal of the retained testicles. (Aren't you guys glad I'm done with that sentence?)

**Famous Pomeranians**

- Queen Victoria had one named "Windsor's Marco."
- Two of the three dogs that survived the sinking of RMS Titanic were Pomeranians. Lady, Miss Margaret Hayes's Pomeranian got away safely in Lifeboat 7. Elizabeth Barrett Rothschild's Pomeranian survived in Lifeboat 6.

(A Pekingese was the other, I knew you were wondering.)

**Verdict**

Not an iceberg's chance in hell.

Pomeranian
S.S. TITA

# Poodle

## *(Arrogantus maximus)*

**Points To Consider**

The Poodle is a breed of water dog which is divided into four varieties: Standard Poodle, Medium Poodle, Miniature Poodle and Toy Poodle. Is that enough for you? The poor Medium Poodle is not universally recognized. Since it's just a small Standard or a large Miniature, it suffers from 'middle child syndrome.' Apparently not every dog has its day.

You know the Poodle, that egotistical snob dog prancing around with its nose in the air—with a name like 'Fifi.'

They can be whelped in several different colors: white, black, brown, blue, gray, silver, cafe au lait, silver beige, cream, apricot and red. (Did you spot the coffee drink in there?).

Now let's talk about grooming. The 'Continental Clip' has the face and rear end clipped leaving tufts of curly hair on the hocks and tip of the tail. The 'Sporting Clip' has the coat evenly clipped over the entire body with the face and paws cut shorter. The reason for the diff…er……. en……………………Oh, geez, sorry, I just nodded off.

**Famous Poodles**

- Winston Churchill and Elvis Presley had poodles.
- Charley, John Steinbeck's poodle in his book, *Travels with Charley*.
- Maybe the Poodle is most famous for being the most popular breed to use for creating hybrids. There are over 40 different Poodle mixes or 'doodles.' Goldendoodle, Labradoodle, Schnoodle, Cockapoo, Shih Poo, Newfypoo and Poochon just to name a fewdle. What, no Xoloitzcuintadoodle.

**Verdict**

Abso-doodley not!

Standard
(ahem,)
Poodle

# Portuguese Water Dog

## *(Aguapuppae iberia)*

**Points To Consider**

The Portuguese Water Dog is a working dog that was originally bred in Portugal. (I didn't see that coming.) They were taught to herd fish into fishermen's nets, retrieve lost tackle or broken nets, and act as couriers from ship to ship or from ship to shore. Kind of like a Portuguese version of a Passenger Pigeon, only wetter and smellier.

The Portuguese Water Dog (gad that's a long name to type every time) loves the water and uses his back legs to swim using its powerful tail as a rudder. Caution: A congenitally curved tail can cause one to swim in circles.

They can have curly coats or wavy coats (like there's a difference?) which can be cut in a 'lion' cut or a 'retriever' cut. Did anyone ask the lions and retrievers about this?

The Portuguese Water Dog (Darn, just typed the whole thing again) has a multi-octave voice. Therefore, his irritating barking can B sharp or B flat.

**Famous Portuguese Water Dogs**

- U.S. President Obama and his family had two Portuguese Water Dogs, Sunny and Bo.
- Snagger Beck of Louisiana had one who rescued all of his lost lures. He had a heck of a time getting them out of his lip. Over the years he saved many Dardevles® and Rapalas®. (Just kidding.)

**Verdict**

No. Too long a name and how many ship to shore messages are you going to send anyway?

Portuguese Water Dog

# Pug

## *(Lapdogus enormitae)*

**Points To Consider**

1) A breed in the Toy Group from China. (A long time ago.)
2) Wrinkly, short muzzled face and curved tail. (Clean wrinkles often to prevent skin fold dermatitis.)
3) By far the largest of the Lap Dogs. (Better have a large lap!)
4) Two distinct ear shapes, 'rose' and 'button.' ('Button' is greatly preferred, don't even think of getting a 'rose-eared' one.)
5) Coats can be fawn, apricot fawn, silver fawn or black. (What color is fawn, anyway? Bambi was camouflaged, maybe it's a color one can't see.) There is a trace of a black line from the occiput to the tail. (Couldn't they just say back of the head?)
6) A sedentary life can lead to Pug obesity. (How unique is that?)
7) Susceptible to Demodectic Mange caused by ubiquitous parasitic mites. (Get off my lap, NOW!)
8) Prone to Brachycephalic Airway Obstructive Syndrome AND Pharyngeal Gag Reflex or reverse sneezing. (Where does the sneeze come out, anyway?)

Conversely, there are also many negative factors.

**Famous Pugs**

The *Men in Black* film series featured 'Frank' a talking Pug. At least Will Smith and Tommy Lee Jones thought he was famous. (See this movie if you haven't, it's a "Scream!")

**Verdict**

Ugh!

*(Illustration à la Edvard Munch)*

Pug

# Rhodesian Ridgeback

## *(Corduroy zimbabwae)*

**Points To Consider**

The Rhodesian Ridgeback is in the Hound Group and was bred in Southern Africa. They are named for the country in which they originated and for the ridge of hair running along the back, in the opposite direction of the coat. A ridge of hair, running backwards? Wow! I think they may be the most like 'Punk Rockers' of all the breeds.

When I first heard of them, I thought they could be found hanging around big ridges…like impact crater rims or glacial moraines or volcanic crater/caldera rims…but no! It's only a ridge of hair on the back.

Their color should be light wheaton to red wheaton. What the heck color is wheaton? I thought he was the actor who played Wesley Crusher on *Star Trek: TNG* or a city in Illinois. Apparently, it's a yellow to beige to rust to reddish to orangish to auburn color. Pretty specific there, right?

To be in conformance, a Rhodesian Ridgeback should have a nose that is black or liver colored. No other colored nose is permissible. Who likes a brown-noser, anyway?

**Famous Rhodesian Ridgebacks**

None surfaced in a brief search. I even asked Tor, my Uber driver. A famous ridge however, is 'Angels Landing,' a hiking trail in Zion National Park. This ridge hike is not for the meek.

**Verdict**

However you say 'No' in Chibarwe, Kalanga, Koisan, Nambya, Ndau and Ndebele—some of the many official languages of Zimbabwe.

Note: In 1980 Rhodesia achieved its independence from Britain and the country's name was changed to Zimbabwe (for you curious geographistory people.)

Rhodesian
Ridgeback

# Rottweiler

## *(T-boneum schlepperhund)*

**Points To Consider**

Rottweil is an old city in southwest Germany which gave the breed its name. The Rottweiler is a working dog that was known in Germany as 'Rottweil Metzgerhund' meaning 'butcher's dog.' Its main use was to herd livestock and pull carts laden with butchered meat to market. (I can't even remember the last time we used our meat cart.)

A Rottweiler is always black with clearly defined markings of a rich tan on the cheeks, muzzle, throat, chest and legs as well as over both eyes and under the base of the tail.

The Rottweiler is also a herding dog and when working cattle, searches out the dominant animal and challenges it. Upon proving its control over that animal, it settles back and tends to its work. Rottweilers will sometimes use their bodies to physically force a stubborn animal to do its bidding. (Note: Don't cross a Rottweiler when he's working.)

It seems Rottweilers have gotten a bad reputation from their depiction in movies as vicious. Or maybe because they are pushy and dominant?

**Famous Rottweilers**

In the city of Rottweil, many years ago, they realized they had only one female dog remaining to continue the breed. Starting with her, using careful techniques, they were able to create a continuous breeding program. A bronze statue of her stands in Rottweil today.

**Verdict**

I'm going to have to exert all of my NO muscle on this one.

Rottweiler

# Russell Terrier

## (Caninus johnrussell)

### Points To Consider

I don't know why this breed is called Russell Terrier rather than Jack Russell Terrier, and I'm too lazy to find out. I'm going to call it Jack Russell Terrier. Take that AKC!

This guy was first bred in England by Reverend John 'Jack' Russell, a parson and hunting enthusiast. He was good at bolting foxes out of their burrows. (The dog, not Rev. John.)

The breed is hunt-driven and will pursue creatures of any kind, including skunks. Unfortunately, the Russell Terrier is prone to Skunk Toxic Shock Syndrome in which the skunk spray causes the red blood cells to undergo hemolysis and can lead to anemia, kidney failure and death.

Before you consider this breed, ask yourself "How many times will I go fox hunting in skunk-free areas?" My money is on not too many!

They have high energy and drive requiring lots of exercise, therefore, are not recommended for apartments or condos. Well, duh!

### Famous Russell Terriers

There are many famous Jack Russells, including 'Eddie' from the TV series *Frasier*. But my favorite is 'Nipper' born in 1884 and is thought to be the inspiration for the painting Dog looking at and listening to a Phonograph which was later named His Master's Voice. The painting was used in advertisements by many music related companies.

### Verdict

Hit The Road, Jack!

Russell
Terrier

# Saint Bernard

## *(Holierthanus thou)*

**Points To Consider**

The Saint Bernard is a GIANT dog classified in the Working Group (if you can call carting a keg of brandy around 'working.') Sounds like a party host to me.

The legend of Saint Bernards carrying brandy in kegs around their necks has been contradicted and thought to be hyperbole. So maybe it was whiskey?

They were bred in the western Alps by monks at the Great Saint Bernard Pass Hospice on the border between Italy and Switzerland and were used for avalanche rescue work. That's laudable.

Realistically, how much time are you planning to spend in the Alps? Outdoors? In avalanche season? If you're still thinking 'nice pet,' remember, they weigh 140-180 pounds, take up the entire couch, eat a lot, lotsa hair, mucho slobber, (***) dog's nose at crotch level. Can you really afford an extra-large pooper scooper? ($$$)

**Famous Saint Bernards**

(This is my favorite 'famous' dog in the book, check out his name!)

'Barry' is the most famous Saint Bernard ever. He reportedly saved 40-100 lives while on duty in the Great Saint Bernard Pass in the Alps. There is a monument to Barry in the Cimetiere des Chiens (dog cemetery) in France and his body was preserved in the Natural History Museum in Bern, Switzerland. What a dog!

**Verdict**

No, Non. Nein. (Have a nice snifter of brandy, instead.)

HAIR
OF THE
DOG
Saint
Bernard

# Saluki

## *(Hundus carbondale)*

**Points To Consider**

Salukis were originally bred in the Fertile Crescent, a region in the middle east spanning Iraq, Syria, Lebanon, Israel, Palestine, Jordan and northern Kuwait. Some people include Cyprus and northern Egypt. Whoa, this is turning into another geography lesson. OK it's a banana-shaped, Mideastern good-farming region.

Salukis are long-legged and narrow sighthounds. So narrow they are easy to spot from the side but almost impossible to see head-on.

The Guinness Book of Records names the Saluki the 'Fastest Dog.' Take that you Greyhounds. Eat our dust.

Salukis do not enjoy rough games or activities such as retrieving balls, but do enjoy soft toys. (Ooooh, I almost didn't have the Nerf® to include this.)

So, if you come across a yard with many un-fetched tennis balls and a racetrack around the house, you could surmise that a Saluki lives there, but you can't see him because he's looking straight at you.

**Famous Salukis**

This one is sooooo easy. By far the most famous Saluki is the mascot of Southern Illinois University in Carbondale. The Saluki has been the mascot since 1951 when it was changed from the Maroons. Good move, SIU!

**Verdict**

No, by the narrowest of margins.

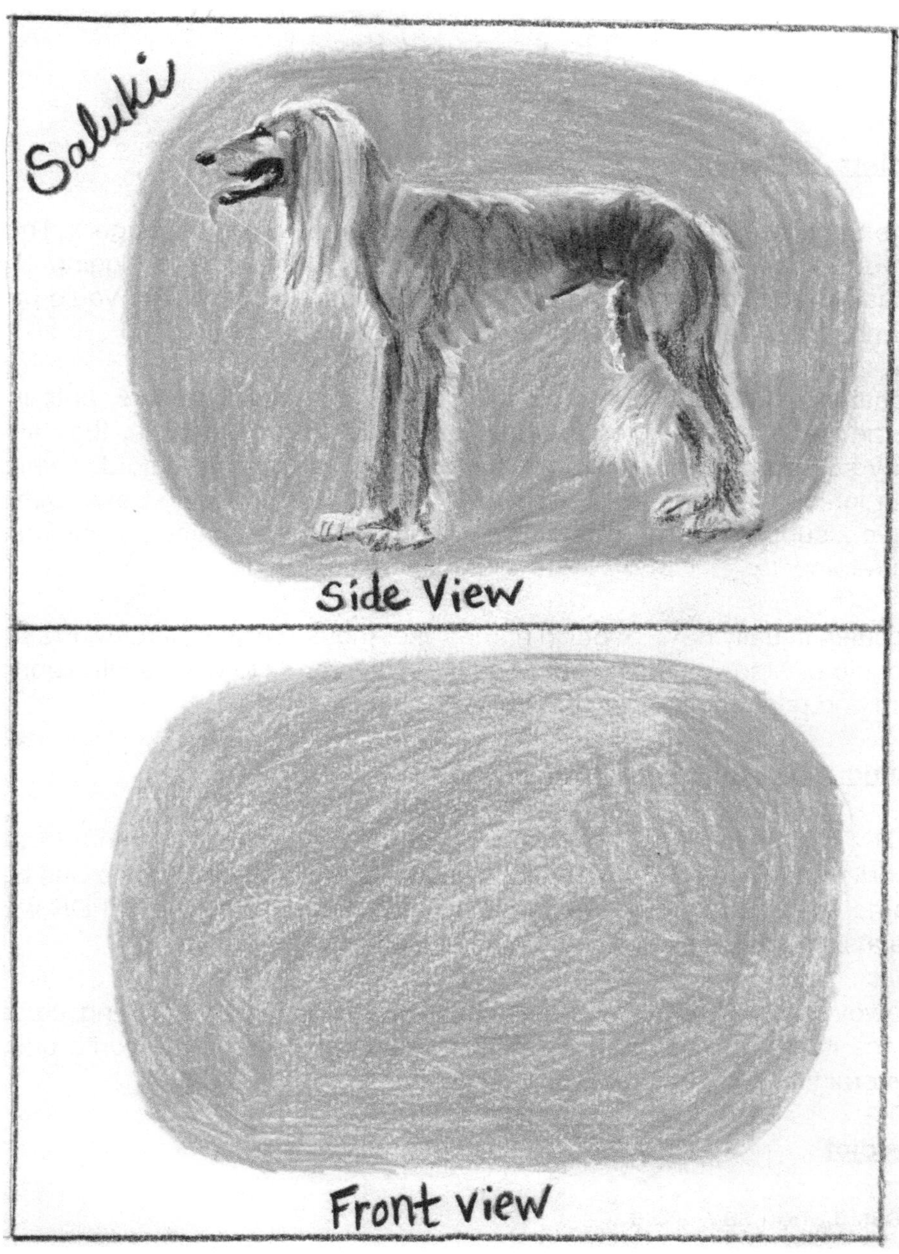
Saluki
Side View
Front view

# Scottish Terrier

## *(Bagpipus kiltae)*

**Points To Consider**

The Scottish Terrier was bred in Scotland to hunt and fight badgers. They are territorial, alert, quick-moving and feisty. Also prone to digging and chasing small mammals such as squirrels, rats and mice. So, you'd better not keep cats, rabbits or ferrets in the same home.

Scotties are susceptible to bleeding disorders, joint disorders, auto-immune diseases, allergies and cancer. If that weren't enough, they also may suffer from Scotty Cramp, an autosomal recessive disorder which can inhibit the dog's ability to walk, if it is under unusual stress. Better have a supply of Valium® and Prozac® available or a canine psychologist on retainer.

Scotties usually have Scottish names like Angus, Fergie, Barclay, Fraser, Bonnie or Mackie. The owner should also be ready to wear a kilt, sport a tam and take bagpipe lessons.

**Famous Scottish Terriers**

U.S. Presidents' dogs are always famous. (Knock me over with a tartan scarf.) 'Fala' was U.S. President Franklin D. Roosevelt's Scottie and became so famous that in Washington, D.C., there is a statue of FDR with Fala sitting at his side. Every dog has its day.

However, my favorite famous Scottie is the Monopoly® playing piece. Since its introduction in the 1950s, it has been voted the favorite piece several times.

**Verdict**

Nessie and I say, "Nae."

*(Illustration à la Andy Warhol)*

Scottish Terrier

# Shih Tzu

## *(Feces menageri)*

**Points To Consider**

This breed was developed in China and is considered a toy dog. But it's alive!

Very small, able to sit in your lap, sometimes called a lap warmer. You'd be better off putting a blanket in the dryer for a few minutes and using that to snuggle up.

By the way, it's pronounced "sheed-zoo." Don't get caught saying "shitz-oo" in polite company.

Apparently, this breed has a plethora of health issues stemming from possible poor breeding over the years. Hip dysplasia, patellar luxation, cataracts, progressive retinal atrophy, retinal detachment, corneal dryness, ear infection, skin allergies and rashes, and my favorite, excessive discharge around the eyes.

Be prepared to spend much of your time at the veterinarian's office. ($$$) Maybe consider a 'standing appointment.'

**Famous Shih Tzus**

There are no famous Shih Tzus. Only famous Shih Tzu owners. I'd name them here but you can find them on the cover of the tabloids at the grocery store check out.

**Verdict**

I'd call off these dogs. Get some sweet and sour pork and wonton soup instead.

Shih Tzu

# Sled Dogs

## (*There are so many)

**Alaskan Husky** *(Martinus buser)*
**Alaskan Malamute** *(Sewardus folly)*
**Siberian Husky** *(Barren oblivion)*

**Points To Consider**

Yes, these are the dogs that pull dog sleds, hence the name 'Sled Dogs.'

It seems that some purebreds don't have blue eyes and some hybrids do. It's all very confusing genetically-speaking (I'm no canine geneticist, nor a rocket scientist, nor a brain surgeon, but I do like to use 'nor' in a sentence.)

So, if you see a Sled Dog with blue eyes, he's probably a canine love child.

**Famous Sled Dogs**

- Yukon King was the dog in the 1950s TV series *Sergeant Preston of the Yukon*. He was an Alaskan Malamute and purportedly pulled a sled for the good sergeant.
- Balto and Togo, two hero sled dogs that participated in the 1925 diphtheria serum run to save victims in Nome, Alaska. This event was the inspiration for the Iditarod race.

**Verdict**

No, I'm not pulling for these guys.

*Also included but not mentioned above are: Samoyed, Greenland Dog, Labrador Husky, McKenzie River Husky, Chinook, Canadian Eskimo Dog, Chukotka Sled Dog, Sakhalin Husky and Yakutian Laika.

Actually, I guess any dog can pull a sled.

Siberian
Husky

# Terrier, Airedale

## *(Inflatus baloonii)*

**Points To Consider**

The Airedale Terrier was bred by working men and miners in the Aire Valley in Britain to be tough and devil-may-care. It is the largest of the British terriers and has earned the title 'King of the Terriers.' Its versatility is legendary. Jobs held by Airedales include: ratter, duck dog, big-game hunter, herder, guardian, warrior, actor, athlete, K-9 cop, and babysitter. (Now that's versatile. No junkyard dog there.)

Versatility aside, they are often judged poorly in AKC conformation shows. This confirms that "To Aire is Human!"

The AKC breed standard states that the correct coat color is tan with a black saddle or a dark grizzle saddle. 'Grizzle' is a mix of colors and should not be confused with 'gristle,' which is what they usually eat.

Two Airedale Terriers were lost in the sinking of the *RMS Titanic*. One was 'Kitty' belonging to John Jacob Aster IV. The other belonged to the Carters of Pennsylvania. (Apparently not quite enough aire in them at the time.)

**Famous Airedale Terriers**

- Ruff, owned by the Mitchell family of *Dennis the Menace* cartoon fame.
- John Wayne's dog, 'Duke,' who gave John his nickname.

**Verdict**

No, easily drownable.

Airedale
Terrier
(River Aire)

# Weimaraner

## *(Grau hund)*

**Points To Consider**

Talk about GREY! The Weimaraner was bred to hunt large or small prey and is named after the city of Weimar in Germany. It is sometimes referred to as the 'Grey Ghost' of the dog world because of its ghostly coat and eye color along with its stealthy hunting style. The eyes are ghostly and the ears long and velvety. The coat can be charcoal, blue, grey or silver. A black coat is an absolute automatic disqualification in dog shows but a small amount of white in the chest area is permitted. (How magnanimous.)

A Weimaraner is an energetic hunting dog prized for its physical endurance and prey-drive. It may tolerate cats but usually doesn't and is likely to kill any small animal. So, if your neighbor's tricolor Persian wanders into your vegetable garden, it won't have been curiosity that killed the cat when you find a calico carcass in your kohlrabi.

They are prone to bloat or gastric torsion, a serious condition. To prevent having a bloated Weimaraner, just don't get one.

**Famous Weimaraners**

Photographer William Wegman had Weimaraners. He photographed them in quirky poses while in human-like costume. The Smithsonian described his photographs as smart, gently subversive humor that parodies all things familiar. (Not my thing, but if this is your cup of tea, it's probably Earl Grey.)

**Verdict**

No grey area here. Not Gonna Happen!

Weimaraner

# Whipped

## *(Devo aurumrecordum)*

**Points To Consider**

The Whippet is a British breed of medium-sized sighthound. The name comes from an early 17th century word meaning 'to move briskly.' They are the fastest dog of their weight (with props to the Greyhounds and Salukis.) Whippets can reach speeds up to 35 mph because of their ability to run in a 'double suspension' gallop. This gait is difficult to explain. I'm going suspend any attempt.

Whippets have been called both a 'poor man's greyhound' and a 'poor man's racehorse.' The heart of a Whippet is large and slow beating, often being arrhythmic or even intermittent when at rest (Could it be Afib?) A 'poor man's veterinarian' might become erroneously concerned.

Many colors of Whippets are allowed: black, white, red, fawn, blue or cream, but not merle. These mottled, piebald dogs with patches of color are, alas, only a 'poor man's whippet.'

(How many times will he use poor man's?)

René Descartes characterized the whippet with the phrase "Grabbafrisbo, ergo sum." Translated from the Latin it is "I catch a Frisbee®, therefore I am."

**Famous Whippets**

Not unexpectedly, only Devo's Gold Record.

**Verdict**

What a troublesome dog is the Whippet,
To a greyhound he's just a snippet,
He'll tip it or nip it or rip it,
A poor man would say "just skip it."

WHAM-O
Whippet

# Xoloitzcuintli

## *(Perro pelón mexicano)*

**Points To Consider**

Now, whoever entered the name for this breed obviously had his fingers on the wrong keys to start. If your fingers are only one key off, to the right or to the left, the expected typed word will be all screwed up, like the name of this breed.

To check if this were the problem, I typed the breed name with fingers off one key to try to find the actual name. To the right I got CP;POYXVIO-MY;R...nope. To the left...ZIKIUR(shift)XYUBRKW...not that either.

Incidentally, Fido would be (off right) Gofp....(off left) Dusi.
Toto would be Ypyp or Riri.
Rin Tin Tin would be Tom Yom Yom or Eub Rub Rub, but I digress.

I found this breed is named after two words in the Nahuatl (southern Mexico) language: Xolotl (God) and Itzcuintli (dog). God is dog spelled backwards, but apparently not in Nahuatl.

This 'Mexican Hairless' breed is characterized by duality, wrinkles and dental abnormalities along with a primitive temper. Oh boy, let's get a wrinkly, psycho dog with bad teeth, shall we? (Bad teeth? Better keep a doggie dentist on retainer.) ($$$)

Life span is 13-18 años. That's a long time to pay for dental work ($$$).

**Famous Xoloitzcuintlis**

Google search yielded cero results. (In 6,587.4 segundos)

**Verdict**

See *Chihuahua*

EL BARBERO
?
Xoloitzcuintle

# Conclusion

# A Case for NOT Owning a Dog

Now that you have been 'Exposed' to 50 different breeds of dogs, you'll see that no dog is the best breed and remains my recommendation. I'm like a dog with a bone about this. If you are still considering getting one, I'd call off the dogs.

Forrest Gump said, "Life is like a box of chocolates, you never know what you're gonna get." Dogs, however, are not like a box of chocolates, you do know what you're going to get; an expensive ($$$), messy (***) pet and no chance for spontaneity. (No spontaneity, that's a big one.)

If you still have 'Puppy Love,' consider this fact. If someone is selling activated charcoal products to be placed inside your house to adsorb dog odors (and they are), this should give you paws.

Thanks for listening. Bye for now. I've got to go see a man about a dog.

# Glossary

(The author offers explanations and definitions for certain words found in this book and other words which are common about dogs or books or anything else, just for fun.)

**A Crapella:** Picking up dog doo without musical accompaniment.
**Ad Nauseam:** How this glossary goes on.
**AKC:** American Kennel Club. They know everything about dogs.
**Alphabetical Order:** The breed list and this glossary are in it.
**Alpha Dog:** Fraternity for Beagles.
**Alliteration:** Calling canines cute and cuddly.
**Alp-O:** Dog food brand from the Swiss mountains.
**Andy Warhol:** Pop art 'Campbell's Soup Can' magnate.
**Appendix:** A small pouch attached to the large intestine.
**Area of a Triangle:** Triangles are in 'geometry.'
**Arf:** Quieter than a bark.
**Au:** Chemical symbol for gold (Latin: Aurum) Elemental, my dear Watson.
**Au Contraire:** "My dog is friendly and doesn't bite."
**Au Courant:** I have a feeling we're not in Kansas anymore.
**Au Gratin:** I'm grateful I don't have a dog.
**Auf Wiedersehen:** See au revoir.
**Au Jus:** Meat gravy for your Kibbles 'n Bits®.
**Au Natural:** Xoloitzcuintli.
**Au Revoir:** See auf wiedersehen.
**Author:** The guy who writes the stuff in the book.
**Badger:** Mascot of the University of Wisconsin, "Go Bucky!"
**Bark:** Louder than an arf.
**Barking Dog:** The one that won't bite? Not to my way of thinkin'.
**Bay:** To bark with prolonged tones at an inlet of the sea.
**Beethoven:** The guy who told Tchaikovsky the news.
**Beg:** To implore, e.g. I beg you not to bring your dog over.
**Bernard:** Bernice, Bernadette and Benedict's brother.
**Binding:** What cheese can be.

**Bite:** Less worse than a bark.
**Blitzkrieg:** Donner's sleigh-pulling mate in Germany.
**Bona Fide:** Fido's bone.
**Bone:** Smallest numbered space on a Bingo card.
**Bon Voyage:** A trip without a dog.
**Bow Wow:** Rapper Shad Gregory Moss.
**Brindle:** The color of 'Jack,' the dog on *Little House on the Prairie*.
**Canina Non Grata:** All dogs in my world.
**Canines:** Long pointed teeth, also called cuspids or FANGS!
**Caninophilia:** Dog people have it.
**Caninophobia:** That's me!
**Caninoambivalence:** (I just made that one up.)
**Capeesh:** Italian for "do you understand?" Capeesh?
**Carpe Diem:** I caught an oily, bottom-feeding fish…today.
**Cat:** A jazz musician.
**Caveat Emptor:** Beware of running out of gas.
**Cave Canem:** Latin for Beware the Dog!
**Chapter:** What the sun and wind did to the cowgirl.
**Chili Dog:** Similar to a Coney Dog, or the Mayor of Santiago.
**Chuckle:** A small throw or toss.
**Chow Chow:** An Italian reiterating his departure.
**Coney Dog:** Similar to a Chili Dog, or a Brooklyn Councilman.
**Coren, Stanley:** Author of *The Intelligence of Dogs*.
**Cougar:** Older than a fox.
**Coursing:** Triple dipping all the appetizers.
**Cover:** What you should do after you duck.
**Crapper:** That little building way out back.
**Cul-De-Sac:** That plastic bag full of dog doo.
**Cur:** Worthless dog; mongrel.
**Daisy:** Dukes of Hazzard cousin
**Déjà vu:** Your dog just farted, AGAIN!
**De Rigueur:** Not humping my leg.
**Dingo:** Star drummer for the Deatles.
**Dino:** Fred and Wilma Flintstone's 'Dog.'
**Disgusting:** To mooch a smooch from a pooch.
**Docked Tail:** Dog's tail that has been cut short. Yelp!
**Dog:** You're reading this book, and you don't know what a dog is?
**Dog and Pony Show:** Toto and Mr. Ed starring in *The Hound of Music*.
**Dog Biscuit:** Canine cousin of the racehorse, Seabiscuit.
**Dog Catcher:** Teammate of the Dog Pitcher.
**Dog Collar:** Person who repeatedly shouts the dog's name.
**Dog Day Afternoon:** A BM in the PM, bring a plastic bag.

**Dog Days:** Every day! You never get a day, if you have a dog.
**Dog Discipline:** Speak softly and carry a big stick.
**Doge:** Venetian chief magistrate.
**Dog Ear:** Miniature corn on the cob.
**Dog Eat Dog:** Odie snacking on some Puppy Chow®.
**Dog Face:** Here's looking at you, kid.
**Dog Food:** That lazy kid's homework.
**Dogg:** Rapper/actor Snoop.
**Doggerel:** The contents of this book.
**Doggie non grata:** Any dog at my house.
**Doggone:** What I wish for every time I see a pet canine.
**Doggy Bag:** Euphemism for 'tomorrow's lunch.'
**Dog House:** Where I spend lots of my time.
**Dogie:** A motherless calf that 'gets along.'
**Dog Leg:** Watch out when he lifts it.
**Dog License:** Permission to use a fire hydrant.
**Doggie Food Bowl:** A food serving device that tips over and spills. (***)
**Doggie Water Bowl:** The toilet.
**Dogma:** Strong doctrine or belief, like 'Dogs usually smell.'
**Dognapping:** What canines do in a dog house.
**Do-gooder:** A dog owner picking up with a plastic bag.
**Dog Paddle:** A trot in the water.
**Dog Park:** WATCH YOUR STEP!
**Dog Pound:** 1/7 of a human pound, or is it seven times?
**Dogs:** A tired person's feet. See John Candy in *Planes, Trains…*
**Dog's Age:** Today's date minus the date he was born. Sheesh!
**Dog's Chance:** The odds I'll get a canine pet.
**Dog's Life:** Anyone with a pet leads one.
**Dog Star:** Sirius, brightest star in the constellation, Canis Major.
**Dog Tag:** Chasing game where one dog is 'It.'
**Dog The Bounty Hunter:** Duane Chapman.
**Dog Tired:** Duane Chapman at the end of the day.
**Dogwood:** Blondie Bumstead's husband.
**Doo:** Don't.
**Double Jeopardy:** Raining cats *and* dogs.
**Drop:** Suggestion to a college student failing a course.
**Drool:** What boys do while girls rule.
**Edvard Munch:** Best-selling Norwegian brand of trail mix.
**Elizabethan Collar:** Nabbing a perp in late 1500s, England.
**England:** Where perps were nabbed in the late 1500s.
**En Masse:** How the perps were nabbed.
**Epilogue:** This book doesn't have one.

**Errata:** TNTC in this book.
**Et Cetera:** He sheds, he pees, he smells, he drools, ...
**Euphemism:** Calling your pet's crap, "Dog Doo."
**Fait Accompli:** You've already stepped in it.
**FCI:** Fédération Cynologique Internationale...everything about dogs, also.
**February 29:** Extra day to pick up dog doo that year.
**Fetch:** Bring me a beer, honey.
**Fido:** Accounting inventory evaluation method; 'First In, Den Out.'
**Firehouse Dog:** Flaming hot habanero/jalapeno wiener in a bun.
**Fire Hydrant:** To pee or not to pee, that is the question.
**Flatulence:** Fancy way of saying farting. Stay upwind from Buster.
**Fleas:** Wool of the golden winged ram that Jason and the Argonauts stole.
**Fox:** Younger than a cougar.
**Genus/Species:** Ultimate taxonomic levels (except for subspecies.)
**Giggle:** A very small group of geese.
**Glory Hound:** Avid fan of the 1989 Denzel Washington movie.
**Glossary:** You're reading one right now.
**Grizzle:** An immature brown bear.
**Guard Dog:** Football position located inside Tackle Dog.
**Guffaw:** Ha Ha, you stepped in it.
**Haiku:** The sound of a Japanese dog sneezing.
**Hair:** 1960s Tribal Love-Rock Musical featuring the song *Aquarius.*
**Hair Ball:** Trichobezoar. Anyone for a good retching session?
**Hair of the Dog:** Missing element on a Xoloitzcuintli.
**Heel:** What a physician is expected to do.
**Helminthologist:** One studying parasitic worms, squirming yet?
**Herding Group:** Group of dogs that herd, duh.
**Hilarity:** Dog owner thinking his dog understands him.
**Hot Dog:** Not a poodle.
**Hound:** Harass, persecute or pursue.
**Hound Dog:** Elvis Presley's 1956 Hit Song.
**Hound Group:** Group of dogs that doesn't herd.
**Howl:** The sound of a hound in a pound.
**Humor:** Best Over-The-Counter medicine. (Laughter is Rx.)
**Hush Puppy:** Ineffective term to quiet a barking dog.
**Hydatid Cysts:** Cystic echinococcosis (tapeworms found in dogs.)
**Ibid:** I'm Being Inundated with Dogs.
**Illustrator:** The person who draws clever, heartwarming and appealing dogs.
**Index:** This book doesn't have one. You're on your own.

**Introduction:** Bowser's trouser check.
**In Vino Veritas:** Tequila tonight, tomorrow we ride!
**Irony:** I actually don't mind dogs that much.
**Jackal:** A dog you don't want an 'introduction' to.
**Je Ne Sais Quoi:** Dogs don't have it.
**Jesus:** Heard right after someone steps in dog-doo.
**John Candy:** Junior Mints® in the Men's room.
**Jowls:** Winston Churchill's dog.
**Junkyard Dog:** Bad, Bad Leroy Brown's pooch.
**K:** Vitamin involved in the blood clotting process.
**K:** Short form of OK for *very* lazy texters.
**K-1:** IRS Form for reporting pass-through income.
**K-2:** Also-ran, runner-up for the highest mountain on earth.
**K-9:** Homophone of canine, K?
**K/9:** A pitcher's average number of strike-outs per nine innings.
**$K_9P$:** Chemical formula for dog urine.
**K-12:** Elementary school, middle school and high school.
**K-99:** Country music radio station in Fort Collins, CO.
**K-abob:** Word following Shish.
**K-Boom:** A large explosion.
**K-Cups:** Single serve coffee. Or a very large brassiere.
**K-Mart®:** American retail company with a blue-light special.
**K-Pop:** Korean popular music.
**K-State:** University in Manhattan, Kansas. Go Wildcats!
**K-Swiss:** Athletic footwear for a Bernese Mountain Dog.
**K-tel®:** Company selling music compilations and the Veg-O-Matic®.
**Kennel:** A large crate or cage to use for ignoring your dog(s).
**Kerfuffle:** Can develop when two dogs are wearing the same sweater.
**Lady:** It's over when the fat one sings.
**Lap Dogs:** The ones too short to drink out of the toilet.
**Lassie:** What the Scottish laddies call their lady friend.
**Laughter:** The best medicine.
**Lead Dog:** The only dog with a different view.
**Leash:** Dog's way of controlling the owner.
**Leathers:** Large pendulous ears or lederhosen. Ach du Lieber!
**Levity:** A southpaw.
**Lincoln Logs:** Abe's memoirs.
**Lucky Dog:** The one that isn't mine.
**Mad Dogs:** "Bitches? We don't need no stinking bitches!" types.
**Mad Dogs and Englishmen:** Those who go out in the midday sun.
**Man's Best Friend:** Woman.
**Maw:** Paw's wife.

**Mea Culpa:** Lead singer for the rock group Yo Guilty Girls.
**Mensa:** Many Educated Nerds Sitting Around.
**Merle:** Songwriter, musician, guitarist and singer, Haggard.
**Mini-Me:** Pint-sized dog owner with a teacup chihuahua.
**Modus Operandi:** That 'pick up' procedure with the plastic bags.
**Monet:** Dog owner who only gives the '*impression*' she's picking up doo.
**Mongrel:** Most dogs.
**Mount Everest:** What the Cavalry Sgt. shouted at Cpl. Everest.
**Mr. Rogers:** Roy, Fred, Kenny or Will, but not Ginger.
**Mutt:** See Mongrel above.
**Muzzle:** The open end of the barrel of a firearm.
**Nessie:** Imaginary creature—like a perfect dog.
**Neuter:** OUCH!
**Non-Sporting Group:** A group of dogs wearing casual clothing.
**Not On Your Nelly:** British for "there is no chance of that happening."
**Occam's Razor:** Philosophy; the simplest explanation is usually the best.
**Oedipup Rex:** Sire of Rex the Wonder Dog.
**Old Yeller:** Maw.
**Onomatopoeia:** Arf, Bark, Bowwow, Grrrr, Yip.
**Oy Vey:** Your dog just barfed.
**Pant:** One half of a pair of trousers.
**Paraphernalia:** Trappings regarded as superfluous, e.g. dog costumes.
**Parody:** What the word 'odd' has.
**Paw:** Maw's husband.
**Pet Store:** Where you buy trappings regarded as superfluous.
**Picasso:** Spanish brand of pooper-scooper.
**Pinscher:** Tight Fittin' Jeans.
**Plague:** The Bubonic Plague, spread by infected fleas on dogs.
**Pluto:** The outermost solar system planet, or is it?
**Pooch:** In golf, a stroke that hits more turf than ball.
**Printer:** A young pupil who hasn't learned cursive yet.
**Publisher:** Arthur Mae Publishing LLC.
**Puke:** A technicolor upchuck. (Alimentary, my dear Watson.)
**Pulitzer Prize:** Award that doesn't have a Humor category.
**Pun:** Many failed attempts in this book.
**Puppet:** Female newborn dog.
**Puppeteer:** Jim Hensen, creator of the Muppets®.
**Puppy:** Beginning stage of dog problems.
**Puppy Love:** Song written/sung by Paul Anka, circa 1960.
**Pup Tent:** A shelter too small for a Great Dane.
**Pyrenees Mountains:** A border between Spain and France.

**References:** People willing to lie about you on a résumé.
**René Descartes:** Device with wheels for groceries during inclement weather.
**Renner, SD:** A community in Minnehaha County, South Dakota.
**Reservoir Dogs:** Posh pedicure establishment.
**Retail Store:** Place to get a 'docked tail' fixed.
**Retriever:** The one who 'goes and gets,' again and again.
**Rex the Wonder Dog:** I wonder how he got the name.
**Rin Tin Tin:** The sound of a lawn mower engine trying to start.
**Roll Over:** What Chuck Berry asked Beethoven to do.
**Rover:** A fourth outfielder in baseball or softball.
**Ruff:** The dog's answer to every question you ask.
**Rule of Paw:** Don't mess with Maw!
**Saliva:** *See* 'Disgusting.'
**Sarcasm:** That sweater looks good on your dog.
**Sea Dog:** Captain Ahab.
**Setter:** The sun, every day.
**Shaggy Dogs:** All dogs, except Xoloitzcuintli.
**Shar Pei:** Chinese brand of permanent marker.
**Sic 'em:** Scary phrase for timid non-dog lovers.
**Sick As A Dog:** Retching up skunk intestines.
**Sit:** Large acne blemish.
**Sly Dog:** Rambo's Rottweiler.
**Smile:** The look on your dog's face just before he farts.
**Snafu:** Getting a dog in the first place.
**Snifter:** How the hound tracked the Avon lady.
**Snoopy:** Intrusively inquisitive.
**Sotto Voce:** If only dogs barked this way.
**Spaniel:** One member of the midwestern R&B singing group (1950s).
**Spay:** Commercial competitor to PayPal®.
**Speak:** Said to a dog when thinking he understands you.
**Spitz:** Olympic gold medal swimmer, Mark.
**Sporting Group:** A group of well-dressed dogs wearing their finest outfits.
**Spot:** The amount of tea an Englishman drinks.
**Stay:** A court order confining your dog to a kennel.
**Stray Dog:** My kid just dropped his wiener.
**Subtitle:** Understated; low key.
**Terrier:** Bath towels that are the better cloth.
**Terrier Group:** Dogs that hunt burrowing animals like wombats or meerkats.
**Tête-à-tête:** Meeting meeting of the minds minds.

**The Thin Man:** Asta's owner, Nick Charles.
**Three Dog Night:** Rock band famous for the song, *Joy to The World*.
**Ticks:** Do a full body check for them, after walking your dog.
**Titanic:** Having great magnitude, force or power, or an unfortunate vessel.
**Title:** Duke, Duke, Duke, Duke of Earl.
**Titter:** You're probably doing it right now.
**TNTC:** Too Numerous To Count, a lot, a real lot.
**Tongue In Cheek:** How this book was written.
**Top Dog:** Lhasa Apso on Mount Everest.
**Toto:** International plumbing supply company (Toto®).
**Toy Group:** A bin in the playroom.
**Turd:** One block past 2nd Street in Oslo.
**Two Left Feet:** One reason dogs can't dance well.
**Underdog:** The place to point to a puddle of pee.
**Urine:** What the basketball coach shouts to a player on the bench.
**Van Gogh:** Traffic cop's direction to the small school bus.
**Veni, Vidi, Vici:** I came, I saw, I stepped in it.
**Verse:** What follows, "For better or…" in Germany.
**Veterinarian:** One small doc for dogs, one giant bill for mankind.
**Wag The Dog:** Unimpressive cousin of Rex the Wonder Dog.
**Watch Dog:** Terse direction to a dog-sitter.
**Westminster:** Where Horace Greeley told young men to go.
**Whelp:** Between whelm and when in the dictionary.
**Wit:** The amount I don't care about dog conversations.
**Withers:** Singer/songwriter Bill whose hits include *Lean On Me* and *Use Me*.
**WOOF:** AM radio station in Dog City, AR.
**Woofer:** A bass range audio speaker or an incessantly barking dog.
**Working Group:** Those with jobs.
**Worms:** A city in Germany near Frankfurt.
**Xoloitzcuintli:** A real dog breed, check it out. (Mexican Hairless)
**Yada yada yada:** What many people think when reading this book.
**Yelp:** Dog for "You stepped on my paw!"
**Yip:** One small spasm that adversely affects an athlete while performing.
**Zero:** The chance that the Pulitzer committee will review this book.
**Zilch:** See Zero.

# References

Google

Wikipedia

akc.org

*Webster's Ninth New Collegiate Dictionary*, Merriam-Webster, Springfield, MA

*Best In Show* (Movie-2000), Castle Rock Entertainment, Warner Bros.

*The New Roget's Thesaurus by Norman Lewis*, 1978 Edition, G.P. Putnam's Sons, New York

and

Ibid.
(I'm not sure what it means but I've seen it in reference lists before.)

# Ode to 'Blu'

*By Emily Hansen*

Perhaps a love of dogs is a recessive trait that skipped my dad, waiting around for me. Hurray!

I've had a few dogs in my life, but none more perfect than a handsome husky-shepherd mix named Blu. We went to the pound looking for an older female dog that didn't shed, but instead brought home a 7-month-old male with a double coat of flying fur.

Quiet and still among the cacophony of barking and yips at the pound, Blu pressed himself against the kennel gate while presenting the most precious 'side-eye' I ever did see. We had him home within a couple of hours. And for 10 years he was the most loyal buddy. Quiet, considerate, sweet, regal and smart.

Once, whilst in the throes of raising moody teenagers, I declared Blu the nicest person in our house. He patrolled our yard daily, his undeniable good looks showcased on our corner lot for all to admire. I still chuckle recalling how Blu was famous in our neighborhood. Lots of people knew him, but not his humans.

"Where do you live? Oh! Blu's house!"

Losing him in 2019 pierced my heart such that it didn't ever heal quite right. I'd do it all over again, though! Will I see him again? I don't know, but if I find a rainbow bridge, I'm checking! Thanks, bud. Mwah!

# About the Author

Barry Behnken is a retired pharmaceutical scientist living in Mequon, WI. A curious mind, love of humor and a certain aversion to dogs led to the development of *A Canine Exposé.* When he's not hiking, playing tennis or pickleball, you'll find him solving puzzles, explaining a scientific phenomenon to a disinterested granddaughter or engaging in a pun war with any willing soul.

Contact Barry at arthurmaepublishing@gmail.com.

Made in the USA
Monee, IL
04 April 2024